maranGraphics™ Learn at First Sight™

Lotus® 1-2-3® Release 4 for Windows™

maranGraphics' Development Group

Published in the United States
by Prentice Hall Career & Technology

Telephone: 1-800-223-1360
Fax: 1-800-445-6991

Distributed in Canada
by Prentice Hall Canada

Telephone: 1-800-567-3800
Fax: 416-299-2529

Distributed Internationally
by Simon & Schuster

Telephone: 201-767-4990
Fax: 201-767-5625

SINGLE COPY PURCHASES (U.S.)

Telephone: 1-800-947-7700
Fax: 515-284-2607

maranGraphics™ *Learn at First Sight*™
Lotus® *1-2-3*® *Release 4 for Windows*™

Trademark Acknowledgments

Published by Prentice Hall Career & Technology
A Paramount Publishing Company
Englewood Cliffs, New Jersey 07632

The animated characters are the copyright of maranGraphics, Inc.

Author:
     Ruth Maran

Consultant:
     Jim Hodges

**Cover Design and
Art Director:**
     Jim C. Leung

Illustrator:
     Dave Ross

Screens:
     Béla Korcsog

Technical Consultant:
     Eric Feistmantl

Editor:
     Judy Maran

Film generated on maranGraphics' Linotronic L-330 imagesetter at 2540 dpi resolution.

Acknowledgments

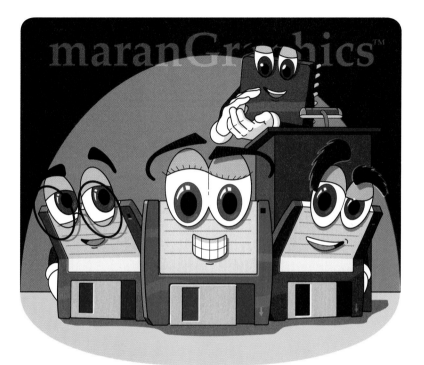

Thanks to Ted Werthman of Prentice Hall Career & Technology for his assistance and creative input.

Special thanks to Jim Hodges of Sheridan College for his assistance in developing the text for this guide. Thanks also to Thierry Mayeur of Lotus Development Canada Ltd. and Saverio C. Tropiano, B.Sc., B.A. for their support and consultation.

To the dedicated staff of maranGraphics including Eric Feistmantl, Béla Korcsog, Jim C. Leung, Jill Maran, Judy Maran, Maxine Maran, Robert Maran, Dave Ross and Monica DeVries-Walraven.

And finally, to Richard Maran who originated the easy-to-use graphic format of this guide. Thank you for your inspiration and guidance.

Table of Contents

 Getting Started

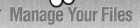 **Enter Data**

Manage Your Files

Formulas and Functions

Spreadsheets produced with pencil, paper and calculator are often time consuming and frustrating. If you change one number in your spreadsheet you may have to redo all of your calculations. This can be a tedious process.

Lotus® 1-2-3® for Windows™ enables you to organize your data and perform calculations in less time and with greater accuracy. If you change a number in your spreadsheet, the program will automatically adjust your results.

Let's Assume...

◆ The Lotus 1-2-3 for Windows program is installed on your hard drive. The default settings are used.

◆ You use a mouse with Lotus 1-2-3 for Windows.

Getting Started	Enter Data	Manage Your Files	Formulas and Functions	Edit Your Worksheet	Format Your Worksheet	Print Your Worksheet	Use Multiple Worksheets	Charts	Databases

Introduction
Mouse Basics
Start Lotus 1-2-3
Lotus 1-2-3 Basics
Move Through a Worksheet

How You Can Use a Spreadsheet

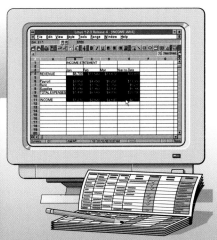

FINANCIAL REPORTS

Businesses of all sizes use spreadsheets to analyze financial information. You can use the formatting and charting features to present your results in a professional looking document.

PERSONAL FINANCES

You can use a spreadsheet to track your personal finances, balance your checkbook, prepare a personal budget, keep track of your mortgage, compare investments and do your taxes.

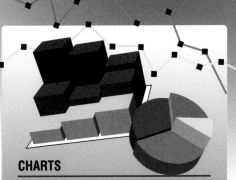

CHARTS

You can create charts directly from your spreadsheet data. Charts visually illustrate relationships between different items.

MOUSE BASICS

The mouse enables you to quickly and easily select commands and perform actions.

Using a Mouse

Hold the mouse as shown in the diagram. Your thumb and two rightmost fingers guide the mouse while your two remaining fingers press the mouse buttons.

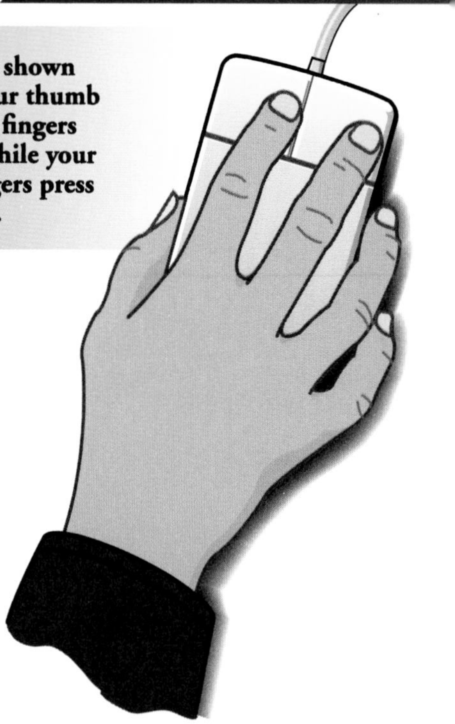

Moving the Mouse Pointer

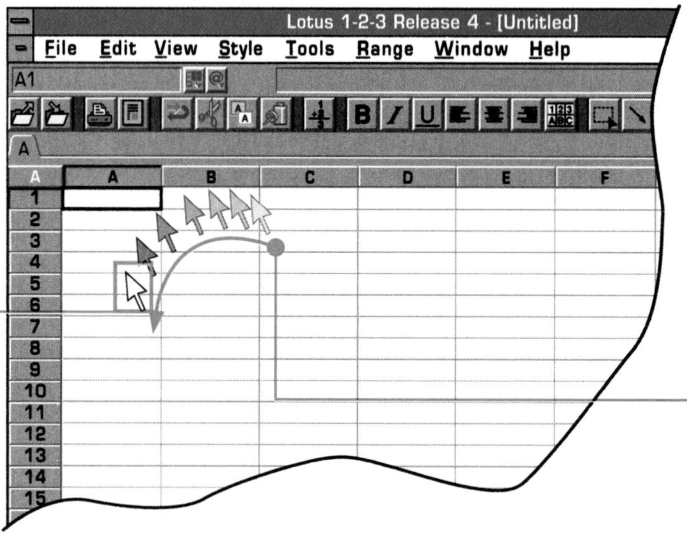
Lotus 1-2-3 Release 4 - [Untitled]
File Edit View Style Tools Range Window Help
A1
A
A B C D E F
1 2 3 4 5 6 7 8 9 10 11 12 13 14 15

◆ The pointer on your screen represents the mouse.

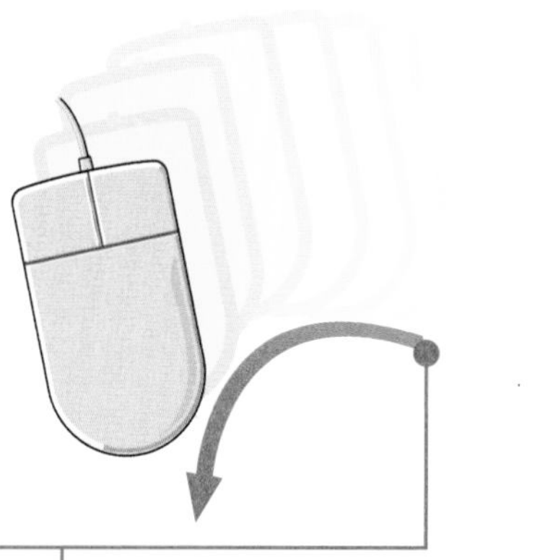

◆ The pointer moves as you move the mouse. For example, the pointer moves down as you move the mouse down.

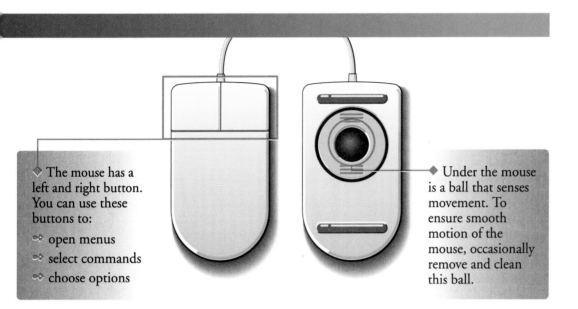

◇ The mouse has a left and right button. You can use these buttons to:

⇨ open menus
⇨ select commands
⇨ choose options

◆ Under the mouse is a ball that senses movement. To ensure smooth motion of the mouse, occasionally remove and clean this ball.

Mouse Terms

TERM	WHAT IT MEANS
Point	Move the pointer ▷ on your screen until it is over the desired object.
Click	Quickly press and release the left mouse button.
Double-click	Quickly press and release the left mouse button twice.
Drag	Press and hold down the left mouse button and then move the mouse.

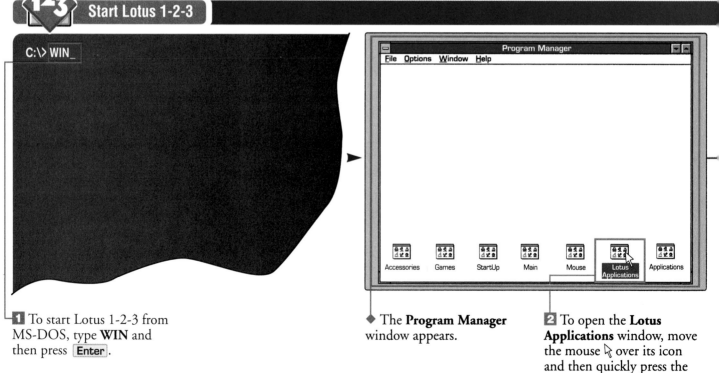

When you start the Lotus® 1-2-3® for Windows™ program, a blank worksheet appears. You can enter your data into this worksheet.

Start Lotus 1-2-3

C:\> WIN_

1 To start Lotus 1-2-3 from MS-DOS, type **WIN** and then press **Enter**.

◆ The **Program Manager** window appears.

2 To open the **Lotus Applications** window, move the mouse ⩱ over its icon and then quickly press the left button twice.

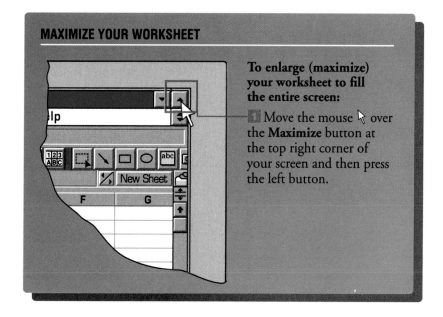

MAXIMIZE YOUR WORKSHEET

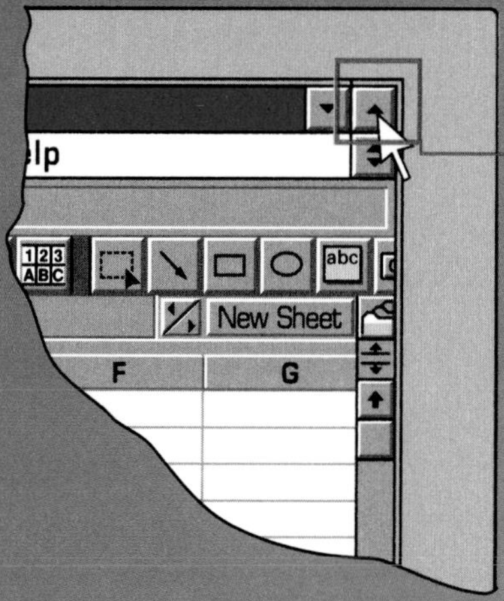

To enlarge (maximize) your worksheet to fill the entire screen:

1 Move the mouse over the **Maximize** button at the top right corner of your screen and then press the left button.

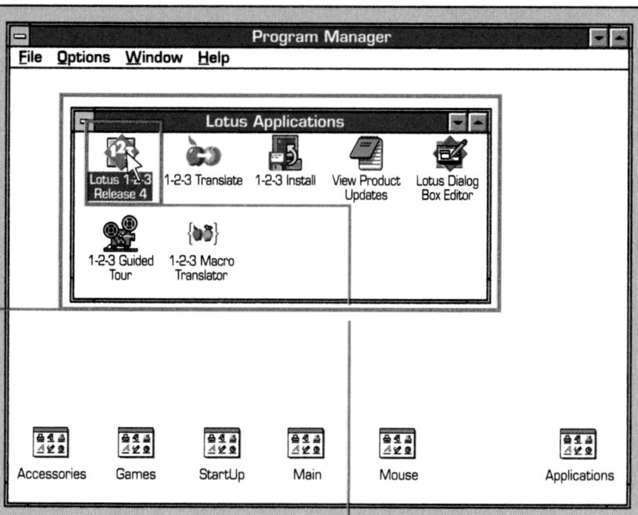

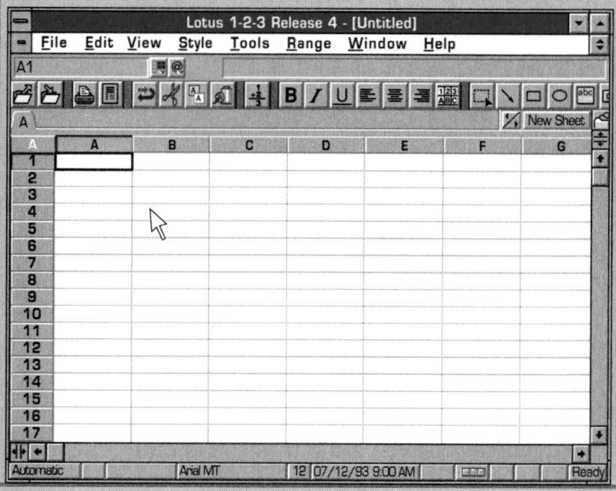

◆ The **Lotus Applications** window appears.

3 To start the **Lotus 1-2-3** application, move the mouse over its icon and then quickly press the left button twice.

◆ The **Lotus 1-2-3** window appears, displaying a blank worksheet.

LOTUS 1-2-3 BASICS

A worksheet consists of rows, columns and cells.

Rows, Columns and Cells

◆ Row

A row is a horizontal line of boxes. The rows are numbered from 1 to 8,192.

◆ Column

A column is a vertical line of boxes. The columns are labeled from A to IV.

◆ Cell

A cell is the area where a row and column intersect.

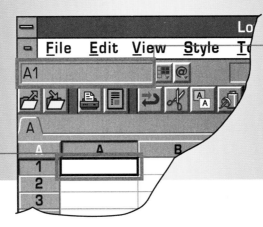

CURRENT CELL

◆ The current cell has a dark border. You can only enter data into the current cell.

CELL ADDRESS

◆ A cell address defines the location of each cell. It consists of a column letter followed by a row number (example: **A1**).

The address of the current cell appears at the top of your worksheet.

SmartIcons enable you to quickly select commonly used commands.

SmartIcons

You can display a description of any SmartIcon.

1 Move the mouse ▷ over the SmartIcon of interest.

2 Press and hold down the **right** mouse button.

◆ A description of the SmartIcon appears at the top of your screen.

3 Release the **right** mouse button to hide the description.

MOVE THROUGH A WORKSHEET

You can use the keyboard or the mouse to move through your worksheet.

To quickly move to any cell on your screen, move the mouse ⊠ over the cell and then press the left button.

Using the Keyboard

MOVE ONE CELL IN ANY DIRECTION

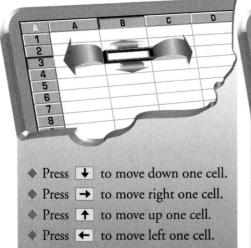

◆ Press ↓ to move down one cell.

◆ Press → to move right one cell.

◆ Press ↑ to move up one cell.

◆ Press ← to move left one cell.

MOVE TO CELL A1

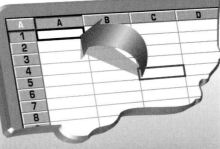

◆ Press **Home** to move to cell **A1** from any cell in your worksheet.

MOVE ONE SCREEN UP OR DOWN

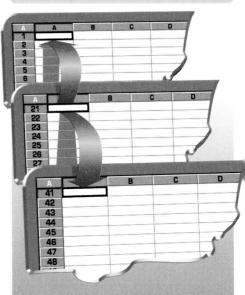

◆ Press **PageDown** to move down one screen.

◆ Press **PageUp** to move up one screen.

Note: Press **Tab** *to move right one screen.*

Press **Shift** + **Tab** *to move left one screen.*

Getting Started	Enter Data	Manage Your Files	Formulas and Functions	Edit Your Worksheet	Format Your Worksheet	Print Your Worksheet	Use Multiple Worksheets	Charts	Databases

Introduction
Mouse Basics
Start Lotus 1-2-3
Lotus 1-2-3 Basics
Move Through a Worksheet

Using the Mouse

SCROLL UP OR DOWN

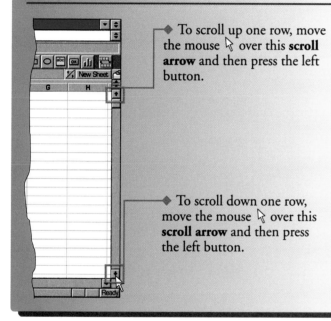

◆ To scroll up one row, move the mouse ⬡ over this **scroll arrow** and then press the left button.

◆ To scroll down one row, move the mouse ⬡ over this **scroll arrow** and then press the left button.

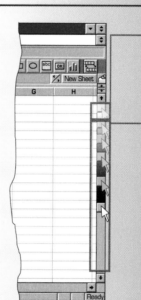

1 To quickly scroll vertically through your worksheet, move the mouse ⬡ over this **scroll box**.

2 Press and hold down the left button and then move the mouse down the **scroll bar**.

3 Release the button.

SCROLL LEFT OR RIGHT

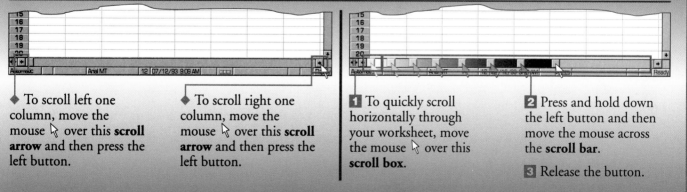

◆ To scroll left one column, move the mouse ⬡ over this **scroll arrow** and then press the left button.

◆ To scroll right one column, move the mouse ⬡ over this **scroll arrow** and then press the left button.

1 To quickly scroll horizontally through your worksheet, move the mouse ⬡ over this **scroll box**.

2 Press and hold down the left button and then move the mouse across the **scroll bar**.

3 Release the button.

ENTER DATA

You can enter both labels and numbers into the cells of your worksheet.

Enter Data

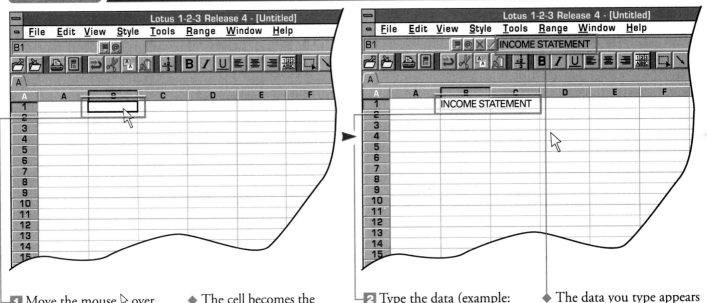

1 Move the mouse ↖ over the cell you want to enter data into (example: **B1**) and then press the left button.

◆ The cell becomes the current cell and displays a dark border.

2 Type the data (example: **INCOME STATEMENT**).

Note: If you make an error typing, press ←Backspace *to remove the incorrect text and then retype.*

◆ The data you type appears in the current cell and at the top of your screen.

Getting Started	Enter Data	Manage Your Files	Formulas and Functions	Edit Your Worksheet	Format Your Worksheet	Print Your Worksheet	Use Multiple Worksheets	Charts	Databases

Enter Data	Fill a Range
Edit Data	Delete Data
Undo	Help
Select Cells	

LONG LABELS

◆ If a label you type is too long to fit in one cell, the text will spill over into adjacent cells if they are empty.

◆ If the adjacent cell contains data, Lotus will display as much of the label as the column width will allow.

Note: To display the entire label, you must widen the column width. For more information, refer to page 48.

LONG NUMBERS

◆ If a number you type is too long to fit in one cell, Lotus will display it in scientific form.

◆ If the exponential form is still too long, asterisks (***) appear in the cell.

Note: To display the entire number, you must widen the column width. For more information, refer to page 48.

ENTERING NUMBERS

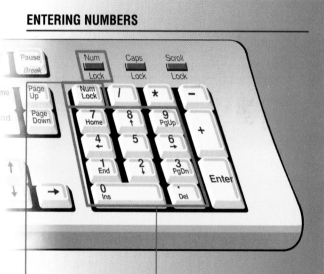

3 To enter the data in the cell, press **Enter**.

or

To enter the data in the cell and move to the next cell, press →, ←, ↓ or ↑.

4 Type and enter the remaining data by repeating steps **1** to **3** for each entry.

◆ You can press **Num Lock** to switch the keys on the right side of your keyboard between number keys and movement keys.

◆ When the **Num Lock** light is on, you can use the numbers 0 through 9 and the decimal point to quickly enter numbers.

◆ When the **Num Lock** light is off, you can use the movement keys to move through your worksheet.

If you discover a typing error in your worksheet, you can easily correct your mistake.

Edit Data

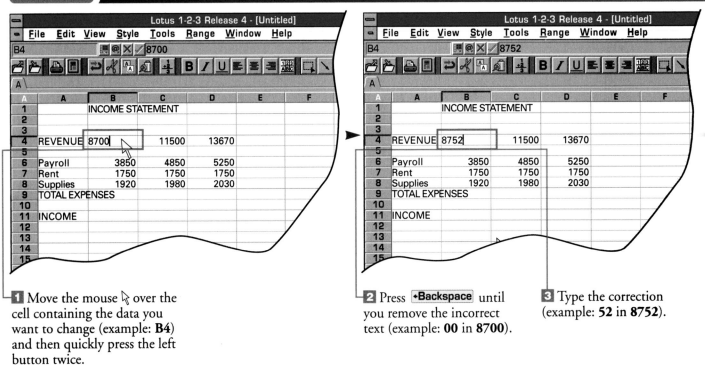

1 Move the mouse ⤢ over the cell containing the data you want to change (example: **B4**) and then quickly press the left button twice.

2 Press **◆Backspace** until you remove the incorrect text (example: **00** in **8700**).

3 Type the correction (example: **52** in **8752**).

Enter Data   Fill a Range
Edit Data   Delete Data
Undo   Help
Select Cells

Undo

Lotus 1-2-3 Release 4 - [Untitled]

File Edit View Style Tools Range Window Help

B4   8700

	A	B	C	D	E	F
1		INCOME STATEMENT				
2						
3						
4	REVENUE	8700	11500	13670		
5						
6	Payroll	3850	4850	5250		
7	Rent	1750	1750	1750		
8	Supplies	1920	1980	2030		
9	TOTAL EXPENSES					
10						
11	INCOME					
12						
13						
14						
15						

You can undo (cancel) your last action or command. This only works immediately after you perform the action.

1 Move the mouse over the **Undo** SmartIcon and then press the left button.

◆ Lotus cancels your last action or command (example: **8752** returns to **8700**).

Lotus 1-2-3 Release 4 - [Untitled]

File Edit View Style Tools Range Window Help

B4   8752

	A	B	C	D	E	F
1		INCOME STATEMENT				
2						
3						
4	REVENUE	8752	11500	13670		
5						
6	Payroll	3850	4850	5250		
7	Rent	1750	1750	1750		
8	Supplies	1920	1980	2030		
9	TOTAL EXPENSES					
10						
11	INCOME					
12						
13						
14						
15						

4 To confirm the change, press **Enter**.

SELECT CELLS

To perform a command on specific cells, you must first select (highlight) them. Selecting cells isolates them so Lotus knows to work with only those cells.

Select a Cell

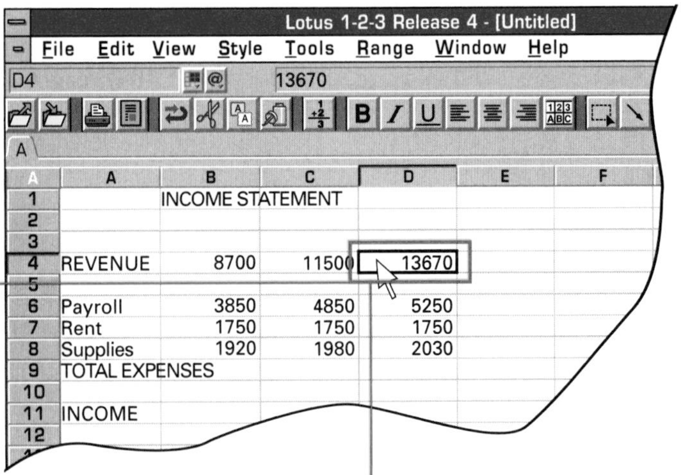
Lotus 1-2-3 Release 4 - [Untitled]
File Edit View Style Tools Range Window Help
D4
13670
A
A B C D E F
1 INCOME STATEMENT
2
3
4 REVENUE 8700 11500 13670
5
6 Payroll 3850 4850 5250
7 Rent 1750 1750 1750
8 Supplies 1920 1980 2030
9 TOTAL EXPENSES
10
11 INCOME
12

1 Move the mouse over the cell you want to select (example: **D4**) and then press the left button.

◆ A dark border appears around the cell to indicate it is the current cell.

Select a Row

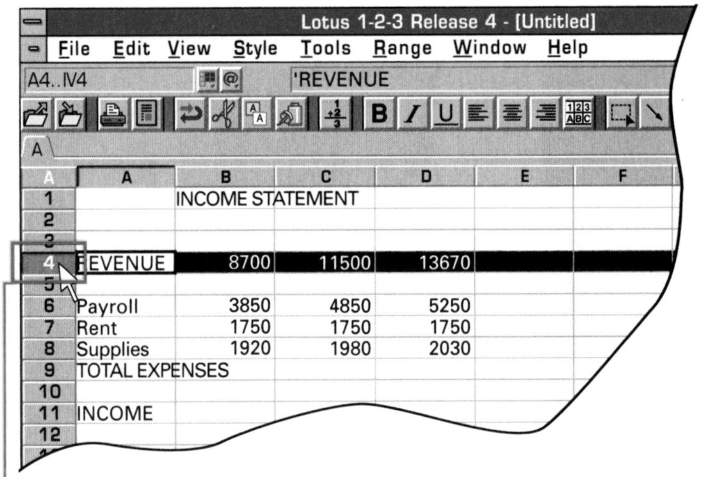
Lotus 1-2-3 Release 4 - [Untitled]
File Edit View Style Tools Range Window Help
A4..IV4
'REVENUE
A
A B C D E F
1 INCOME STATEMENT
2
3
4 REVENUE 8700 11500 13670
5
6 Payroll 3850 4850 5250
7 Rent 1750 1750 1750
8 Supplies 1920 1980 2030
9 TOTAL EXPENSES
10
11 INCOME
12

1 Move the mouse over the row number you want to select (example: **4**) and then press the left button.

Note: Make sure the mouse looks like (not ✥) before pressing the button.

Note: To cancel the selection, move the mouse over any cell and then press the left button.

Enter Data   Fill a Range
Edit Data   Delete Data
Undo   Help
Select Cells

Select a Column

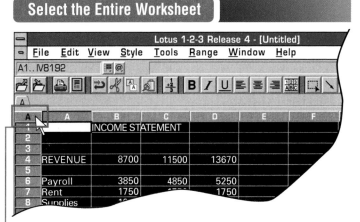

Select the Entire Worksheet

1 Move the mouse over the column letter you want to select (example: **B**) and then press the left button.

Note: To cancel the selection, move the mouse over any cell and then press the left button.

1 Move the mouse over the worksheet letter and then press the left button.

Note: To cancel the selection, move the mouse over any cell and then press the left button.

Select a Cell Range

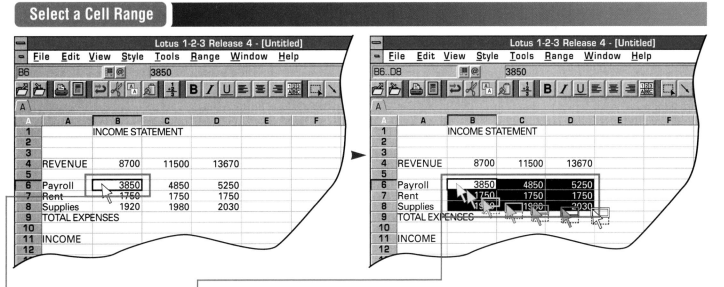

1 Move the mouse over the first cell you want to select (example: **B6**) and then press and hold down the left button.

2 Still holding down the button, drag the mouse until you highlight all the cells you want to select.

3 Release the button.

Note: To cancel the selection, move the mouse over any cell and then press the left button.

SELECT TWO CELL RANGES

To select another cell range, press and hold down Ctrl while repeating steps **1** to **3**.

FILL A RANGE

You can have Lotus complete a pattern of labels or numbers in your worksheet.

Lotus fills cells with a pattern based on the data in the first cell. Some examples are:

Monday	Tuesday	Wednesday	Thursday
Product 1	Product 2	Product 3	Product 4
09:00	10:00	11:00	12:00
1993	1994	1995	1996
Q1	Q2	Q3	Q4

Fill a Range (With Labels)

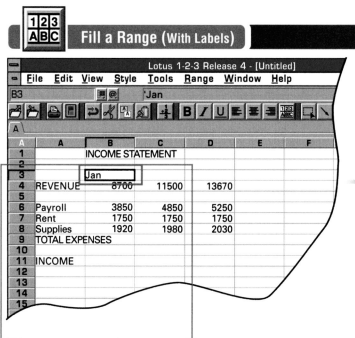

1 Move the mouse ⟶ over the cell you want to contain the first item of the series (example: **B3**) and then press the left button.

2 Type the data (example: **Jan**) and then press **Enter**.

Getting Started	**Enter Data**	Manage Your Files	Formulas and Functions	Edit Your Worksheet	Format Your Worksheet	Print Your Worksheet	Use Multiple Worksheets	Charts	Databases

Enter Data	**Fill a Range**
Edit Data	Delete Data
Undo	Help
Select Cells	

Lotus normally completes a pattern in increments of one unit (example: 1,2,3 or Jan, Feb, Mar).

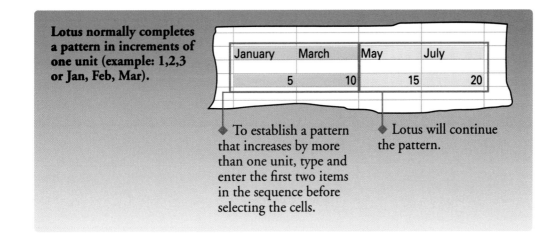

◆ To establish a pattern that increases by more than one unit, type and enter the first two items in the sequence before selecting the cells.

◆ Lotus will continue the pattern.

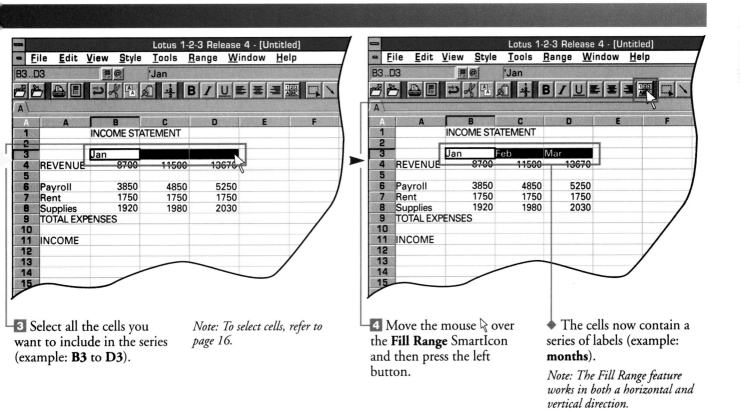

3 Select all the cells you want to include in the series (example: **B3** to **D3**).

Note: To select cells, refer to page 16.

4 Move the mouse ⌕ over the **Fill Range** SmartIcon and then press the left button.

◆ The cells now contain a series of labels (example: **months**).

Note: The Fill Range feature works in both a horizontal and vertical direction.

Fill a Range (With Numbers)

1 Move the mouse ▷ over the cell you want to contain the first item of the series (example: **A13**) and then press the left button.

2 Type the data (example: **1**) and then press **Enter**.

3 Select all the cells you want to include in the series (example: **A13** to **D13**).

Note: To select cells, refer to page 16.

4 Move the mouse ▷ over the **Fill Range** SmartIcon and then press the left button.

◆ The cells now contain a series of numbers.

Enter Data
Edit Data
Undo
Select Cells

Fill a Range
Delete Data
Help

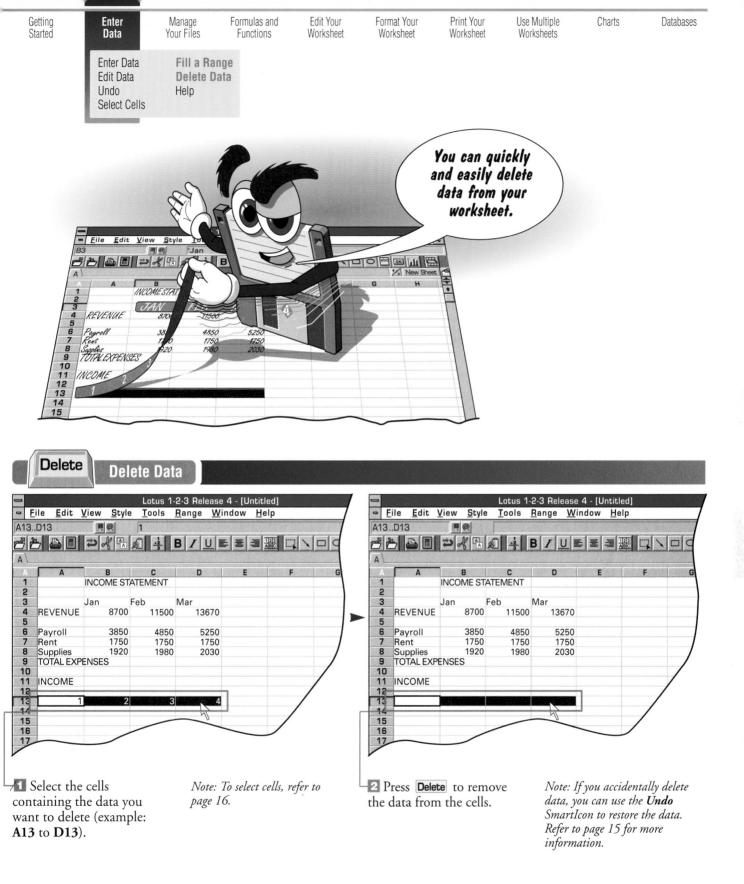

Delete Data

1 Select the cells containing the data you want to delete (example: **A13** to **D13**).

Note: To select cells, refer to page 16.

2 Press **Delete** to remove the data from the cells.

*Note: If you accidentally delete data, you can use the **Undo** SmartIcon to restore the data. Refer to page 15 for more information.*

If you forget how to perform a certain task, you can use the Help feature to obtain information.

Help

1 Move the mouse ⌖ over **Help** and then press the left button. The **Help** menu appears.

2 Move the mouse ⌖ over a topic you want to investigate (example: **How Do I?**) and then press the left button.

◆ The **Help** window appears.

3 Move the mouse ⌖ over a topic of interest (example: **Enter data**) and it changes to ⬏. Then press the left button.

4 To enlarge the Help window to fill your entire screen, move the mouse ⌖ over its **Maximize** button and then press the left button.

Enter Data   Fill a Range
Edit Data   Delete Data
Undo   **Help**
Select Cells

DISPLAY A DEFINITION

In the Lotus 1-2-3 Help window, you can display a definition of any term that appears in green text with a dotted underline.

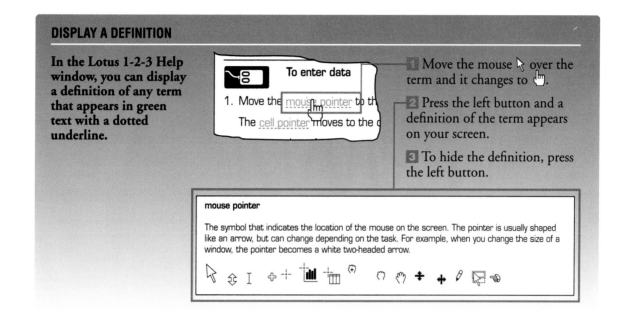

1 Move the mouse over the term and it changes to a hand.

2 Press the left button and a definition of the term appears on your screen.

3 To hide the definition, press the left button.

mouse pointer

The symbol that indicates the location of the mouse on the screen. The pointer is usually shaped like an arrow, but can change depending on the task. For example, when you change the size of a window, the pointer becomes a white two-headed arrow.

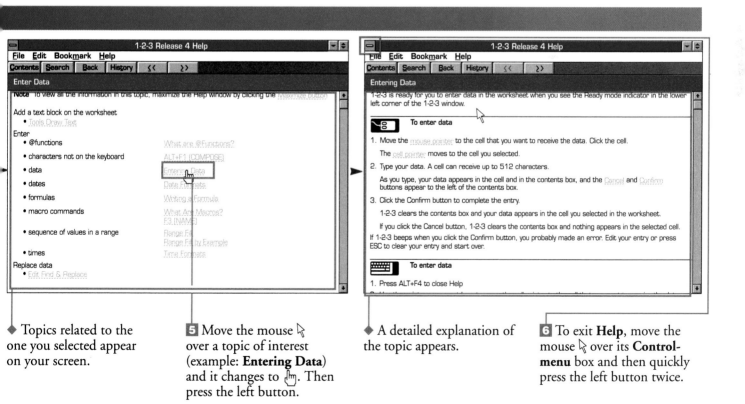

◆ Topics related to the one you selected appear on your screen.

5 Move the mouse over a topic of interest (example: **Entering Data**) and it changes to a hand. Then press the left button.

◆ A detailed explanation of the topic appears.

6 To exit **Help**, move the mouse over its **Control-menu** box and then quickly press the left button twice.

What are Drives?

Your computer stores programs and data in devices called "drives." Like a filing cabinet, a drive stores information in an organized way.

◆ Most computers have one hard drive and one or two floppy drives. The hard drive is called drive C. The floppy drives are called drives A and B.

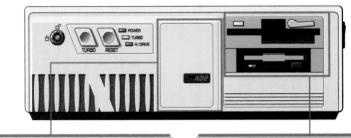

Hard drive (C:)

◆ A hard drive permanently stores programs and data. Most computers have at least one hard drive, called drive **C**.

*Note: Your computer may be set up to have additional hard drives (example: drive **D**).*

Floppy drives (A: and B:)

◆ A floppy drive stores programs and data on removable diskettes (or floppy disks). A diskette operates slower and stores less data than a hard drive.

Diskettes are used to:
* Load new programs.
* Store backup copies of data.
* Transfer data to other computers.

If your computer has only one floppy drive, it is called drive **A**.

If your computer has two floppy drives, the second drive is called drive **B**.

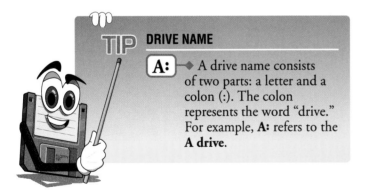

TIP   DRIVE NAME

A: ◆ A drive name consists of two parts: a letter and a colon (:). The colon represents the word "drive." For example, **A:** refers to the **A drive**.

| Getting Started | Enter Data | **Manage Your Files** | Formulas and Functions | Edit Your Worksheet | Format Your Worksheet | Print Your Worksheet | Use Multiple Worksheets | Charts | Databases |

Drives   Save File to a Diskette
Directories   Exit Lotus
Save a New File   Open a File

What are Directories?

◆ Directories

A directory usually contains related information. For example, Lotus automatically stores your worksheet files in the **SAMPLE** directory.

◆ Files

When you save a worksheet, Lotus stores it as a file. You should select a unique and meaningful file name.

Directories are like the drawers and folders in a filing cabinet. They help you organize the programs and data stored in the drives.

SAVE A
NEW FILE

When you finish working on your worksheet, make sure you save it before exiting Lotus. This permanently stores your worksheet for future use.

INCOME.WK4

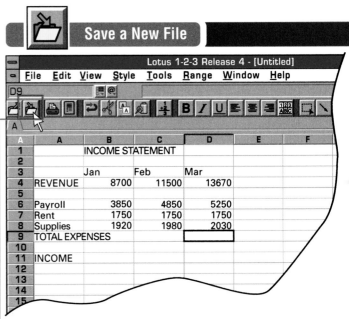

Lotus 1-2-3 Release 4 - [Untitled]

File Edit View Style Tools Range Window Help

D9

B / U

	A	B	C	D	E	F
1		INCOME STATEMENT				
2						
3		Jan	Feb	Mar		
4	REVENUE	8700	11500	13670		
5						
6	Payroll	3850	4850	5250		
7	Rent	1750	1750	1750		
8	Supplies	1920	1980	2030		
9	TOTAL EXPENSES					
10						
11	INCOME					
12						
13						
14						
15						

1 Move the mouse ▷ over the **Save** SmartIcon and then press the left button.

A file name consists of two parts: a name and an extension. You must separate these parts with a period.

INCOME . WK4

◆ **Period**

A period must separate the name and the extension.

◆ **Name**

The name should describe the contents of a file. It can have up to eight characters.

◆ **Extension**

The extension describes the type of information a file contains. It can have up to three characters.

Getting Started	Enter Data	Manage Your Files	Formulas and Functions	Edit Your Worksheet	Format Your Worksheet	Print Your Worksheet	Use Multiple Worksheets	Charts	Databases

Drives   Save File to a Diskette
Directories   Exit Lotus
Save a New File   Open a File

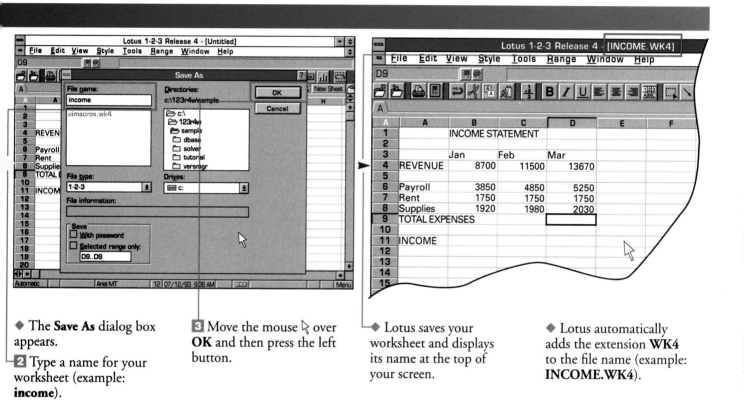

◆ The **Save As** dialog box appears.

2 Type a name for your worksheet (example: **income**).

3 Move the mouse ⌖ over **OK** and then press the left button.

◆ Lotus saves your worksheet and displays its name at the top of your screen.

◆ Lotus automatically adds the extension **WK4** to the file name (example: **INCOME.WK4**).

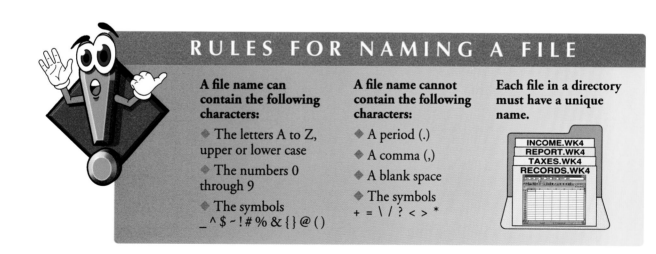

RULES FOR NAMING A FILE

A file name can contain the following characters:

◆ The letters A to Z, upper or lower case

◆ The numbers 0 through 9

◆ The symbols
_ ^ $ ~ ! # % & { } @ ( )

A file name cannot contain the following characters:

◆ A period (.)

◆ A comma (,)

◆ A blank space

◆ The symbols
+ = \ / ? < > *

Each file in a directory must have a unique name.

INCOME.WK4
REPORT.WK4
TAXES.WK4
RECORDS.WK4

SAVE FILE TO A DISKETTE

As a precaution, save your worksheet to a diskette. You can then use this copy to replace any lost data if your hard drive fails or you accidentally erase the file.

Save File to a Diskette

1 Insert a diskette into the appropriate floppy drive.

2 Move the mouse ⟷ over **File** and then press the left button.

◆ The **File** menu appears.

3 Move the mouse ⟷ over **Save As** and then press the left button.

◆ The **Save As** dialog box appears.

◆ The **File name:** box displays the current file name (example: **income.wk4**).

Note: To save your worksheet using a different name, type a new name.

4 To change the current drive (**c:**) to a floppy drive (**a:** or **b:**), move the mouse ⟷ over the arrow in the **Drives:** box and then press the left button.

Drives   **Save File to a Diskette**
Directories   Exit Lotus
Save a New File   Open a File

TIP

◆ After you save your worksheet, you may want to make additional changes. You can use **Save As** to save your revised worksheet with a new name. This way, you still have a copy of the old version in case you regret any changes you made.

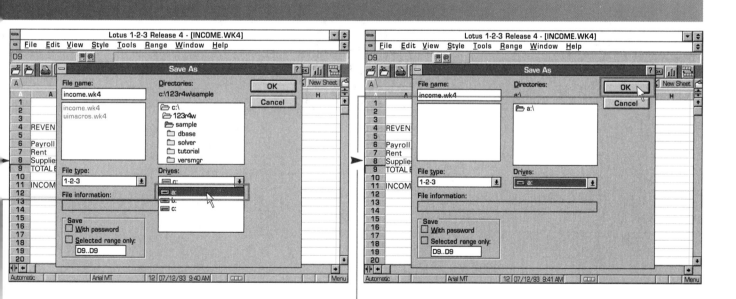

5 Move the mouse ⌖ over the drive you want to use (example: **a:**) and then press the left button.

6 To save your worksheet, move the mouse ⌖ over **OK** and then press the left button.

◆ Lotus saves your worksheet on the selected floppy drive (example: **a:**).

29

EXIT
LOTUS

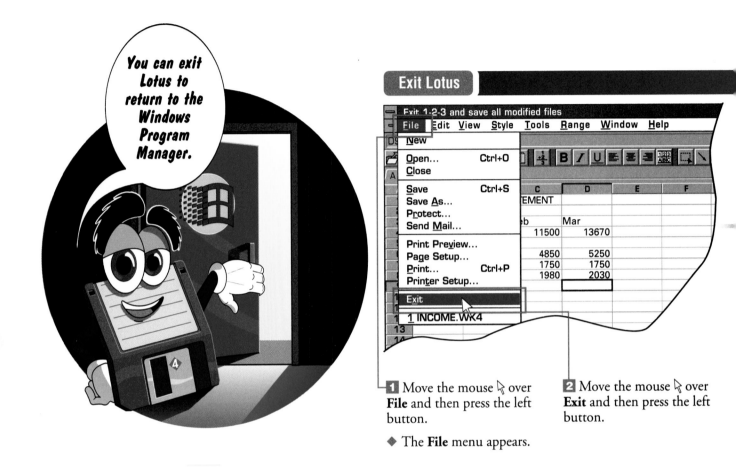

You can exit Lotus to return to the Windows Program Manager.

Exit Lotus

Exit 1-2-3 and save all modified files

| File | Edit | View | Style | Tools | Range | Window | Help |

New
Open...   Ctrl+O
Close

Save   Ctrl+S
Save As...
Protect...
Send Mail...

Print Preview...
Page Setup...
Print...   Ctrl+P
Printer Setup...

Exit

1 INCOME.WK4

	C	D	E	F
	EMENT			
b	Mar			
	11500	13670		
	4850	5250		
	1750	1750		
	1980	2030		

1 Move the mouse over **File** and then press the left button.

◆ The **File** menu appears.

2 Move the mouse over **Exit** and then press the left button.

You must always exit Lotus before turning off your computer. Failure to do so may result in damage or loss of valuable data.

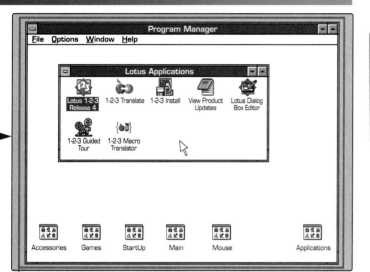

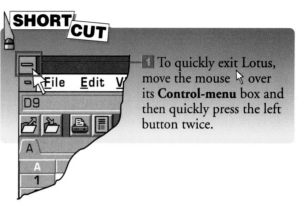

SHORT CUT

1 To quickly exit Lotus, move the mouse ▷ over its **Control-menu** box and then quickly press the left button twice.

◆ The **Program Manager** window appears.

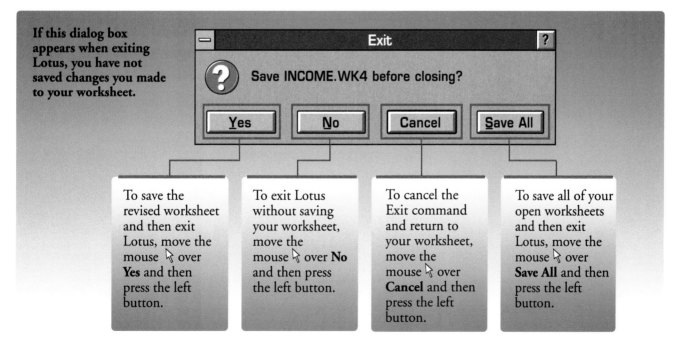

If this dialog box appears when exiting Lotus, you have not saved changes you made to your worksheet.

Exit

? Save INCOME.WK4 before closing?

| Yes | No | Cancel | Save All |

To save the revised worksheet and then exit Lotus, move the mouse ▷ over **Yes** and then press the left button.

To exit Lotus without saving your worksheet, move the mouse ▷ over **No** and then press the left button.

To cancel the Exit command and return to your worksheet, move the mouse ▷ over **Cancel** and then press the left button.

To save all of your open worksheets and then exit Lotus, move the mouse ▷ over **Save All** and then press the left button.

OPEN A FILE

 Open a File

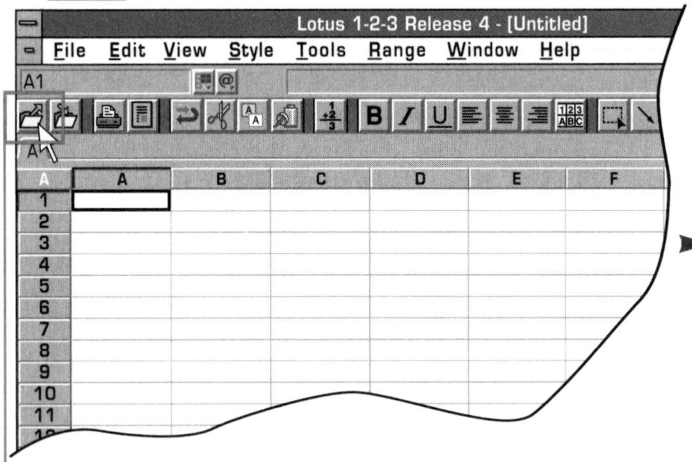

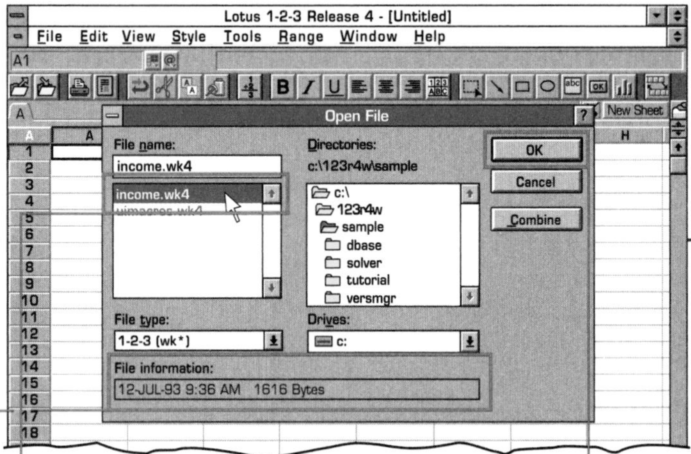

1 Move the mouse over the **Open File** SmartIcon and then press the left button.

◆ The **Open File** dialog box appears.

2 Move the mouse over the name of the file you want to open (example: **income.wk4**) and then press the left button.

◆ The **File information:** box displays the date you last saved the file and its size.

3 To open the file, move the mouse over **OK** and then press the left button.

Getting Started	Enter Data	**Manage Your Files**	Formulas and Functions	Edit Your Worksheet	Format Your Worksheet	Print Your Worksheet	Use Multiple Worksheets	Charts	Databases

Drives   Save File to a Diskette
Directories   Exit Lotus
Save a New File   **Open a File**

OPEN A FILE SAVED ON A DISKETTE

1 Insert the diskette into the appropriate floppy drive.

2 Move the mouse over the **Open File** SmartIcon and then press the left button.

3 To change the current drive (**c:**) to a floppy drive (**a:** or **b:**), move the mouse over the arrow in the **Drives:** box and then press the left button.

Drives:
☐ c: ⬇

4 Move the mouse over the drive you want to use (example: **a:**) and then press the left button.

5 Follow steps **2** and **3** in "**Open a File**" below.

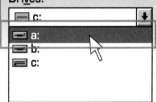

Drives:
☐ c: ⬇
☐ a:
☐ b:
☐ c:

SHORTCUT

Lotus 1-2-3 Release 4 - [INCOME.WK4]

File Edit View Style Tools Range Window Help

D9

	A	B	C	D	E	F
1		INCOME STATEMENT				
2						
3		Jan	Feb	Mar		
4	REVENUE	8700	11500	13670		
5						
6	Payroll	3850	4850	5250		
7	Rent	1750	1750	1750		
8	Supplies	1920	1980	2030		
9	TOTAL EXPENSES					
10						
11	INCOME					

◆ Lotus opens your worksheet and displays it on your screen. You can now make changes to your worksheet.

File
New
Open...   Ctrl+O
Close
Save   Ctrl+S
Save As...
Protect...
Send Mail...
Print Preview...
Page Setup...
Print...   Ctrl+P
Printer Setup...
Exit
1 INCOME.WK4

The File menu displays the names of the last five worksheets you opened. To open one of these worksheets:

1 Move the mouse over **File** and then press the left button.

2 Move the mouse over the name of the worksheet you want to open (example: **INCOME.WK4**) and then press the left button.

FORMULAS

You can use formulas to perform calculations on your worksheet data.

Formulas contain operators. Some examples are:

+	Addition
-	Subtraction
*	Multiplication
/	Division
^	Exponentiation

Lotus performs calculations in the following order:

1 Exponentiation
2 Multiplication and Division
3 Addition and Subtraction

FORMULA	CALCULATION	EXPLANATION
+A1+B1*C1	10+20*5=110	Multiply 20 by 5, then add 10
+A1-B1*C1	10-20*5=-90	Multiply -20 by 5, then add 10
+A1+B1/C1	10+20/5=14	Divide 20 by 5, then add 10
+B1/A1*C1	20/10*5=10	Divide 20 by 10, then multiply by 5
+A1^D1*C1	10^2*5=500	10 to the power of 2, then multiply by 5

A1=10   B1=20   C1=5   D1=2

You can change the order that Lotus calculates your formulas by using brackets ( ). Lotus will calculate the numbers in brackets first.

FORMULA	CALCULATION	EXPLANATION
+A1*B1-C1	10*20-5=195	Multiply 10 by 20, then subtract 5
+A1*(B1-C1)	10*(20-5)=150	Subtract 5 from 20, then multiply by 10
+A1/C1*D1	10/5*2=4	Divide 10 by 5, then multiply by 2
+A1/(C1*D1)	10/(5*2)=1	Multiply 5 by 2, then divide into 10

A1=10   B1=20   C1=5   D1=2

◆ Formulas start with a plus sign (+).

◆ The formula for the current cell appears at the top of your screen (example: **+A1+A2+A3+A4**).

◆ Use cell addresses in formulas instead of numbers whenever possible.

◆ The result of the formula appears in the cell containing the formula (example: **A6**).

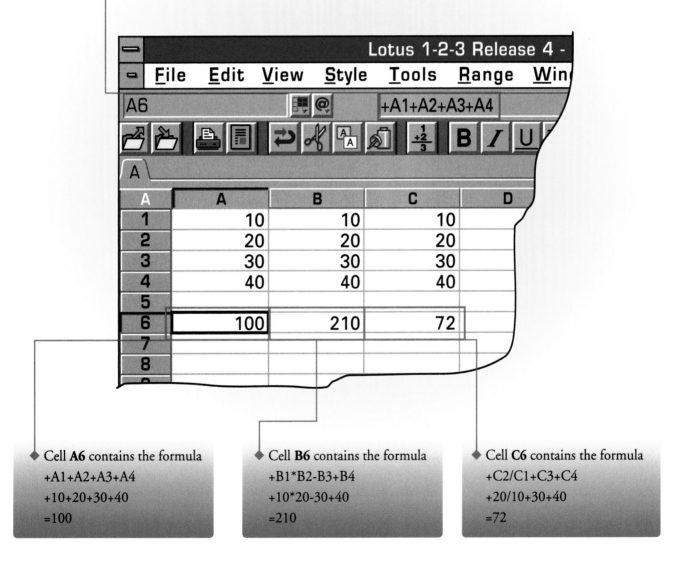

◆ Cell **A6** contains the formula
+A1+A2+A3+A4
+10+20+30+40
=100

◆ Cell **B6** contains the formula
+B1*B2-B3+B4
+10*20-30+40
=210

◆ Cell **C6** contains the formula
+C2/C1+C3+C4
+20/10+30+40
=72

You can enter a formula into any cell in your worksheet.

Enter a Formula

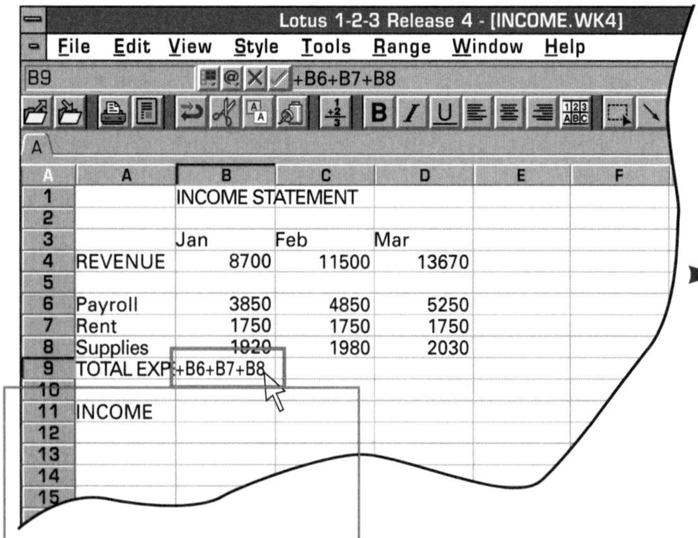

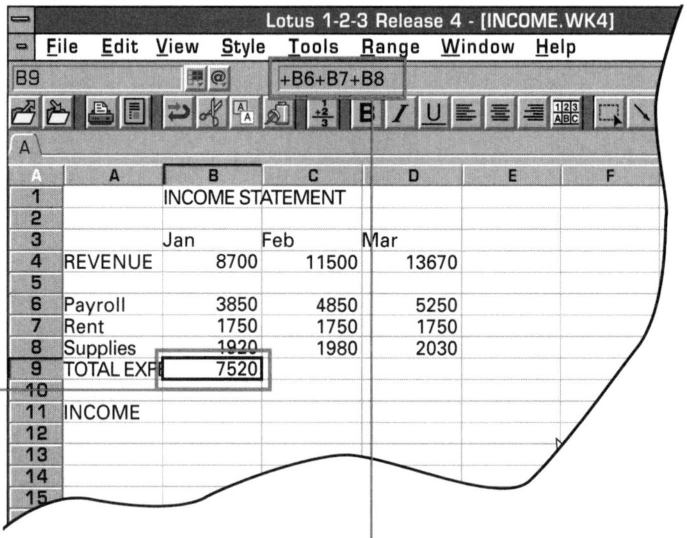

1 Move the mouse � over the cell you want to enter a formula into (example: **B9**) and then press the left button.

2 Type a plus sign (+) to begin the formula.

3 Type the rest of the formula (example: **B6+B7+B8**).

Note: This formula will calculate the Total Expenses for the month of January.

4 Press **Enter** and the result of the calculation appears (example: **7520**).

◆ The formula is displayed at the top of your screen.

Recalculation

Lotus 1-2-3 Release 4 - [INCOME.WK4]

File Edit View Style Tools Range Window Help

B8   @ X / 1890

	A	B	C	D	E	F
1		INCOME STATEMENT				
2						
3		Jan	Feb	Mar		
4	REVENUE	8700	11500	13670		
5						
6	Payroll	3850	4850	5250		
7	Rent	1750	1750	1750		
8	Supplies	1890	1980	2030		
9	TOTAL EXPE	7520				
10						
11	INCOME					
12						
13						
14						
15						

Lotus 1-2-3 Release 4 - [INCOME.WK4]

File Edit View Style Tools Range Window Help

B8   @ 1890

	A	B	C	D	E	F
1		INCOME STATEMENT				
2						
3		Jan	Feb	Mar		
4	REVENUE	8700	11500	13670		
5						
6	Payroll	3850	4850	5250		
7	Rent	1750	1750	1750		
8	Supplies	1890	1980	2030		
9	TOTAL EXPE	7490				
10						
11	INCOME					
12						
13						
14						
15						

If you change a number used in a formula, Lotus will automatically recalculate a new result.

◼1 Move the mouse ⬡ over the cell you want to change (example: **B8**) and then press the left button.

◼2 Type a new number (example: **1890**).

◼3 Press **Enter** and Lotus automatically calculates the new result (example: **7490**).

Lotus provides you with more than **200** built-in formulas, called functions. Functions are ready-to-use formulas that will save you time.

You must tell Lotus what data to use to calculate a function. This data is enclosed in brackets ( ).

@SUM(A1,A3,A4)

♦ When there is a comma between cell addresses in a function, Lotus uses each cell to perform the calculation.

For example, @SUM(A1,A3,A4) is the same as the formula +A1+A3+A4.

@SUM(A1..A4)

♦ When there are two periods between cell addresses in a function, Lotus uses the displayed cells and all cells between them to perform the calculation.

For example, @SUM(A1..A4) is the same as the formula +A1+A2+A3+A4.

Formulas   Sum SmartIcon
Recalculation   Errors
Functions   Copy Formulas

◆ Functions start with the @ symbol.

◆ The function for the current cell appears at the top of your screen (example: **@SUM(A1..A4)**).

◆ Functions cannot contain any spaces.

◆ Use cell addresses in functions instead of numbers whenever possible (example: **A1..A4**).

◆ The result of the function appears in the cell containing the function (example: **A6**).

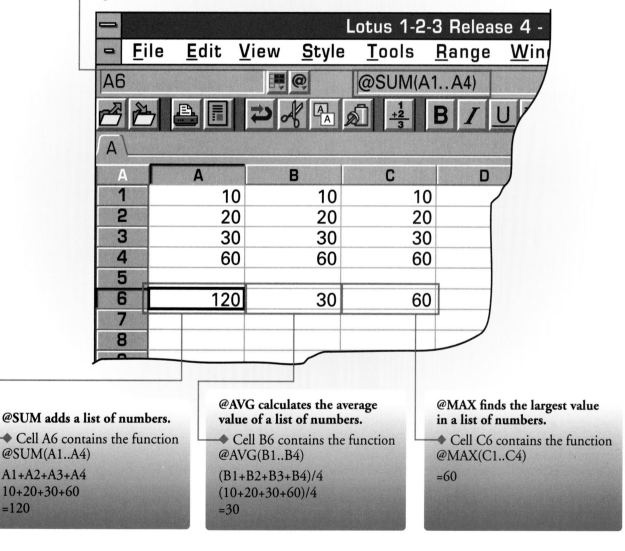

Lotus 1-2-3 Release 4 -

File **Edit** **View** **Style** **Tools** **Range** **Win**

A6   @   @SUM(A1..A4)

A	A	B	C	D
1	10	10	10	
2	20	20	20	
3	30	30	30	
4	60	60	60	
5				
6	120	30	60	
7				
8				

@SUM adds a list of numbers.

◆ Cell A6 contains the function @SUM(A1..A4)

A1+A2+A3+A4
10+20+30+60
=120

@AVG calculates the average value of a list of numbers.

◆ Cell B6 contains the function @AVG(B1..B4)

(B1+B2+B3+B4)/4
(10+20+30+60)/4
=30

@MAX finds the largest value in a list of numbers.

◆ Cell C6 contains the function @MAX(C1..C4)

=60

Once you have selected a function, you must tell Lotus what values to use to produce the final result.

Enter a Function

1 Move the mouse ⌖ over the cell where you want to enter a function (example: **E4**) and then press the left button.

2 Move the mouse ⌖ over the **@function selector** and then press the left button.

◆ A menu appears. It displays the most commonly used functions.

Note: You can select one of these functions and then skip to step **7**

3 To display a list of all the functions, move the mouse ⌖ over **List All** and then press the left button.

4 To display more functions, move the mouse ⌖ over the down or up arrow in the **@Functions:** box and then press the left button.

5 Move the mouse ⌖ over the function you want to use (example: **SUM**) and then press the left button.

6 Move the mouse ⌖ over **OK** and then press the left button.

Getting Started	Enter Data	Manage Your Files	Formulas and Functions	Edit Your Worksheet	Format Your Worksheet	Print Your Worksheet	Use Multiple Worksheets	Charts	Databases

Formulas   Sum SmartIcon
Recalculation   Errors
Functions   Copy Formulas

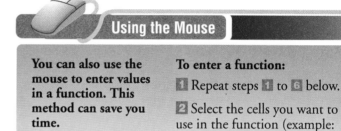

Using the Mouse

You can also use the mouse to enter values in a function. This method can save you time.

To enter a function:

1 Repeat steps **1** to **6** below.

2 Select the cells you want to use in the function (example: **B4** to **D4**).

3 Press **Enter**.

7 Type the cells you want to use in the function (example: **B4,C4,D4**). Make sure you separate each cell with a comma.

*Note: In this example, you could also type **B4..D4**.*

This function will calculate the total Revenue.

8 Press **Enter** and the result of the function appears (example: **33870**).

*Note: The **Year-to-Date** heading was entered into cell **E3**.*

◆ The function is displayed at the top of your screen.

> You can use the SUM SmartIcon to quickly add a list of values in your worksheet.

Sum SmartIcon

In this example, the values in cells B6, C6 and D6 are added together.

1 Move the mouse ⯭ over the cell you want to display the sum (example: **E6**) and then press the left button.

Note: Make sure you select a cell next to the data you want to add together.

2 Move the mouse ⯭ over the **Sum** SmartIcon and then press the left button.

◆ The sum appears (example: **13950**).

◆ The SUM function is displayed at the top of your screen.

Formulas   **Sum SmartIcon**
Recalculation   **Errors**
Functions   Copy Formulas

Errors

ERR (ERROR)

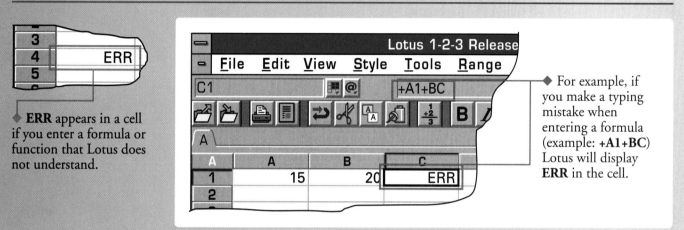

◆ **ERR** appears in a cell if you enter a formula or function that Lotus does not understand.

◆ For example, if you make a typing mistake when entering a formula (example: **+A1+BC**) Lotus will display **ERR** in the cell.

CIRC (CIRCULAR REFERENCE)

◆ If **Circ** appears at the bottom of your screen, a formula or function you entered is incorrect.

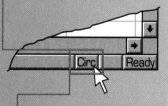

◆ To find the error, move the mouse ♖ over **Circ** and then press the left button. The cell containing the error then becomes the current cell.

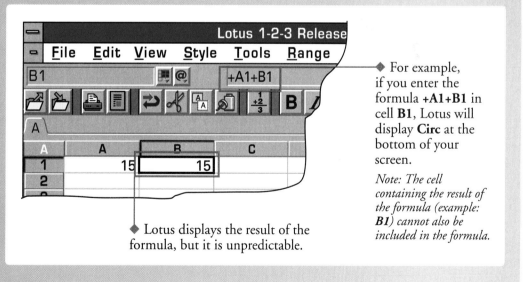

◆ For example, if you enter the formula **+A1+B1** in cell **B1**, Lotus will display **Circ** at the bottom of your screen.

Note: The cell containing the result of the formula (example: B1) cannot also be included in the formula.

◆ Lotus displays the result of the formula, but it is unpredictable.

COPY
FORMULAS

> *You can copy a formula to other cells in your worksheet. Lotus will automatically change the cell addresses for you.*

123 ABC Copy Formulas (Using Relative References)

Lotus 1-2-3 Release 4 - [INCOME.WK4]

File Edit View Style Tools Range Window Help

B9..D9   @   +B6+B7+B8

	A	B	C	D	E	F
1		INCOME STATEMENT				
2						
3		Jan	Feb	Mar	Year-to-Date	
4	REVENUE	8700	11500	13670	33870	
5						
6	Payroll	3850	4850	5250	13950	
7	Rent	1750	1750	1750		
8	Supplies	1890	1980	2030		
9	TOTAL EXPE	7490				
10						
11	INCOME					
12						
13						
14						
15						

Lotus 1-2-3 Release 4 - [INCOME.WK4]

File Edit View Style Tools Range Window Help

B9..D9   @   +B6+B7+B8

	A	B	C	D	E	F
1		INCOME STATEMENT				
2						
3		Jan	Feb	Mar	Year-to-Date	
4	REVENUE	8700	11500	13670	33870	
5						
6	Payroll	3850	4850	5250	13950	
7	Rent	1750	1750	1750		
8	Supplies	1890	1900	2030		
9	TOTAL EXPE	7490	8580	9030		
10						
11	INCOME					
12						
13						
14						
15						

1 Move the mouse ▷ over the cell containing the formula you want to copy (example: **B9**) and then press and hold down the left button.

2 Still holding down the button, drag the mouse until you highlight all the cells you want to copy the formula to (example: **C9** and **D9**).

3 Release the button.

4 Move the mouse ▷ over the **Fill Range** SmartIcon and then press the left button.

◆ Lotus copies the formula and displays the results.

| Getting Started | Enter Data | Manage Your Files | **Formulas and Functions** | Edit Your Worksheet | Format Your Worksheet | Print Your Worksheet | Use Multiple Worksheets | Charts | Databases |

Formulas   Sum SmartIcon
Recalculation   Errors
Functions   **Copy Formulas**

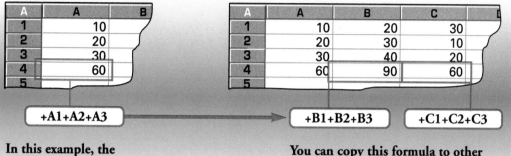

In this example, the formula +A1+A2+A3 was entered into the worksheet.

You can copy this formula to other cells in your worksheet. Lotus will automatically change the cell addresses for you.

5 Move the mouse ⬏ over a cell where you copied the formula (example: **D9**) and then press the left button.

◆ Lotus adjusted the cell addresses when it copied the formula.

◆ You can repeat steps **1** to **4** to copy the formula in cell **E6** to cells **E7**, **E8** and **E9**.

◆ To calculate **INCOME**, you must subtract Total Expenses from Revenue. To accomplish this, enter the formula **+B4-B9** into cell **B11**. You can then repeat steps **1** to **4** to copy this formula to cells **C11**, **D11** and **E11**.

COPY
FORMULAS

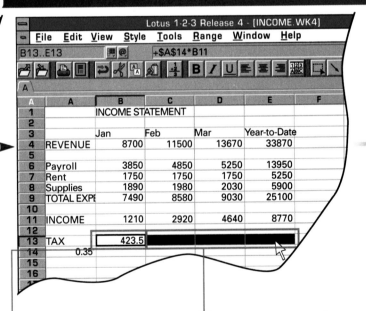

> You can copy a formula to other cells in your worksheet. To keep a cell address fixed, you can instruct Lotus to lock the cell address when copying the formula. This makes the cell reference absolute.

Copy Formulas (Using Absolute References)

Lotus 1-2-3 Release 4 - [INCOME.WK4]

File   Edit   View   Style   Tools   Range   Window   Help

B13   +$A$14*B11

	A	B	C	D	E	F
1		INCOME STATEMENT				
2						
3		Jan	Feb	Mar	Year-to-Date	
4	REVENUE	8700	11500	13670	33870	
5						
6	Payroll	3850	4850	5250	13950	
7	Rent	1750	1750	1750	5250	
8	Supplies	1890	1980	2030	5900	
9	TOTAL EXPE	7490	8580	9030	25100	
10						
11	INCOME	1210	2920	4640	8770	
12						
13	TAX	423.5				
14	0.35					
15						
16						

Lotus 1-2-3 Release 4 - [INCOME.WK4]

File   Edit   View   Style   Tools   Range   Window   Help

B13..E13   +$A$14*B11

	A	B	C	D	E	F
1		INCOME STATEMENT				
2						
3		Jan	Feb	Mar	Year-to-Date	
4	REVENUE	8700	11500	13670	33870	
5						
6	Payroll	3850	4850	5250	13950	
7	Rent	1750	1750	1750	5250	
8	Supplies	1890	1980	2030	5900	
9	TOTAL EXPE	7490	8580	9030	25100	
10						
11	INCOME	1210	2920	4640	8770	
12						
13	TAX	423.5				
14	0.35					
15						
16						

1 Type and enter the data you want to use as an absolute reference (example: **0.35** in cell **A14**).

2 Move the mouse ⇧ over the cell you want to contain the formula with the absolute reference (example: **B13**) and then press the left button.

3 To calculate the tax on your Income, type the formula **+$A$14*B11** and then press **Enter**.

Note: You have defined cell A14 as an absolute reference. Lotus will not change this reference during the copy process.

4 Move the mouse ⇧ over the cell containing the formula you want to copy (example: **B13**) and then press and hold down the left button.

5 Still holding down the button, drag the mouse until you highlight all the cells you want to copy the formula to (example: **C13** to **E13**).

6 Release the button.

Formulas
Recalculation
Functions

Sum SmartIcon
Errors
Copy Formulas

To make a cell reference absolute, type a dollar sign ($) before the column letter and the row number (example: $B$1).

A	A	B	C	D	E
1	Cost per Item	$10			
2					
3	Number of Items	10	20	50	
4	Total Cost	$100	$200	$500	
5					

+$B$1*B3 → +$B$1*C3   +$B$1*D3

In this example, the formula +$B$1*B3 was entered into the worksheet.

You can copy this formula to other cells in the worksheet. Lotus does not change the cell address B1 because it is an absolute reference.

Lotus 1-2-3 Release 4 - [INCOME.WK4]

File Edit View Style Tools Range Window Help

B13..E13   @   +$A$14*B11

A	A	B	C	D	E	F
1		INCOME STATEMENT				
2						
3		Jan	Feb	Mar	Year-to-Date	
4	REVENUE	8700	11500	13670	33870	
5						
6	Payroll	3850	4850	5250	13950	
7	Rent	1750	1750	1750	5250	
8	Supplies	1890	1980	2030	5900	
9	TOTAL EXPE	7490	8580	9030	25100	
10						
11	INCOME	1210	2920	4640	8770	
12						
13	TAX	423.5	1022	1624	3069.5	
14	0.35					
15						

Lotus 1-2-3 Release 4 - [INCOME.WK4]

File Edit View Style Tools Range Window Help

D13   @   +$A$14*D11

A	A	B	C	D	E	F
1		INCOME STATEMENT				
2						
3		Jan	Feb	Mar	Year-to-Date	
4	REVENUE	8700	11500	13670	33870	
5						
6	Payroll	3850	4850	5250	13950	
7	Rent	1750	1750	1750	5250	
8	Supplies	1890	1980	2030	5900	
9	TOTAL EXPE	7490	8580	9030	25100	
10						
11	INCOME	1210	2920	4640	8770	
12						
13	TAX	423.5	1022	1624	3069.5	
14	0.35					
15						
16						

7 Move the mouse ▷ over the **Fill Range** SmartIcon and then press the left button.

◆ Lotus copies the formula and displays the results.

8 Move the mouse ▷ over a cell where you copied the formula (example: **D13**) and then press the left button.

◆ Lotus did not change the absolute reference in the formula (example: **$A$14**). However, Lotus did change the relative reference (example: **D11**).

CHANGE COLUMN WIDTH

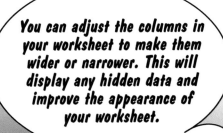

You can adjust the columns in your worksheet to make them wider or narrower. This will display any hidden data and improve the appearance of your worksheet.

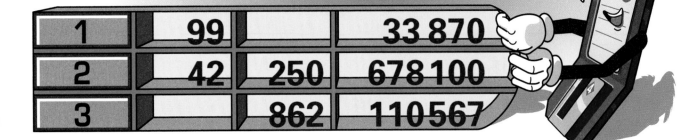

Change Column Width

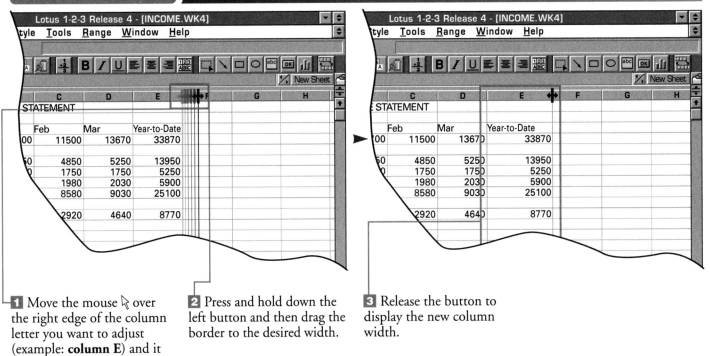

1 Move the mouse ⌖ over the right edge of the column letter you want to adjust (example: **column E**) and it changes to ✛.

2 Press and hold down the left button and then drag the border to the desired width.

3 Release the button to display the new column width.

Getting Started	Enter Data	Manage Your Files	Formulas and Functions	**Edit Your Worksheet**	Format Your Worksheet	Print Your Worksheet	Use Multiple Worksheets	Charts	Databases

Change Column Width
Change Row Height
Insert a Row or Column

Delete a Row or Column
Move Data
Copy Data

Change Column Width Automatically

Lotus 1-2-3 Release 4 - [INCOME.WK4]

File   Edit   View   Style   Tools   Range   Window   Help

A13

	A	B	C	D	E	F
1		INCOME STATEMENT				
2						
3		Jan	Feb	Mar	Year-to-Date	
4	REVENUE	8700	11500	13670	33870	
5						
6	Payroll	3850	4850	5250	13950	
7	Rent	1750	1750	1750	5250	
8	Supplies	1890	1980	2030	5900	
9	TOTAL EXPE	7490	8580	9030	25100	
10						
11	INCOME	1210	2920	4640	8770	
12						
13						
14						
15						

▶

Lotus 1-2-3 Release 4 - [INCOME.WK4]

File   Edit   View   Style   Tools   Range   Window   Help

A13

	A	B	C	D	E
1		INCOME STATEMENT			
2					
3		Jan	Feb	Mar	Year-to-Date
4	REVENUE	8700	11500	13670	33870
5					
6	Payroll	3850	4850	5250	13950
7	Rent	1750	1750	1750	5250
8	Supplies	1890	1980	2030	590
9	TOTAL EXPENSES	7490	8580	9030	25
10					
11	INCOME	1210	2920	4640	
12					
13					
14					
15					

You can have Lotus adjust the column width to fit the longest item in the column.

1 Move the mouse ↖ over the right edge of the column letter you want to adjust (example: **column A**) and it changes to ↔.

2 Quickly press the left button twice.

◆ The column width changes to fit the longest item in the column (example: **TOTAL EXPENSES**).

CHANGE ROW HEIGHT

You can change the height of a row to enhance the appearance of your worksheet.

Change Row Height

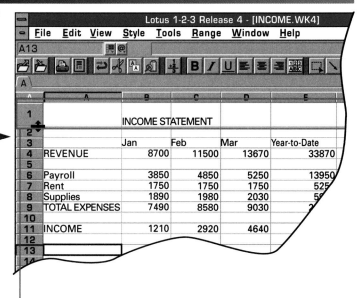

1 Move the mouse ⍭ over the bottom edge of the row number you want to adjust (example: **row 1**) and it changes to ✚ .

2 Press and hold down the left button and then drag the border to the desired height.

3 Release the button to display the new row height.

Getting Started	Enter Data	Manage Your Files	Formulas and Functions	**Edit Your Worksheet**	Format Your Worksheet	Print Your Worksheet	Use Multiple Worksheets	Charts	Databases

Change Column Width   Delete a Row or Column
Change Row Height   Move Data
Insert a Row or Column   Copy Data

Change Row Height Automatically

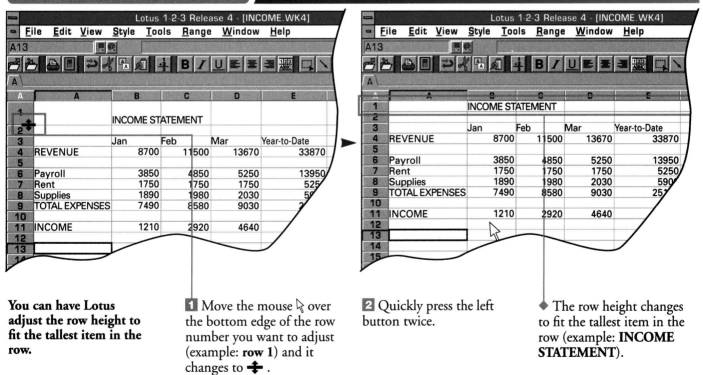

You can have Lotus adjust the row height to fit the tallest item in the row.

1 Move the mouse ⬚ over the bottom edge of the row number you want to adjust (example: **row 1**) and it changes to ✚ .

2 Quickly press the left button twice.

◆ The row height changes to fit the tallest item in the row (example: **INCOME STATEMENT**).

INSERT A ROW OR COLUMN

You can insert a row or column into your worksheet. This allows you to add data you forgot to include.

Insert a Row

Lotus inserts a row above the row you select.

1 To select a row, move the mouse ⬀ over the row number (example: **row 4**) and then press the left button.

2 Move the mouse ⬀ anywhere over the selected row and then press the **right** button. A menu appears.

3 Move the mouse ⬀ over **Insert** and then press the left button.

◆ Lotus inserts a row and shifts all existing data downward.

Getting Started	Enter Data	Manage Your Files	Formulas and Functions	**Edit Your Worksheet**	Format Your Worksheet	Print Your Worksheet	Use Multiple Worksheets	Charts	Databases

Change Column Width   Delete a Row or Column
Change Row Height   Move Data
Insert a Row or Column   Copy Data

TIPS

◆ When you insert a row or column, Lotus automatically adjusts all formulas affected by the insertion.

◆ You can use the **Undo** SmartIcon to delete a row or column you just inserted. This only works immediately after inserting the row or column.

Insert a Column

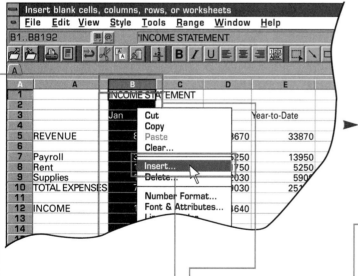

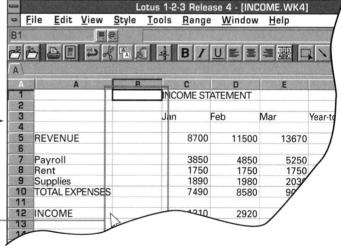

Lotus inserts a column to the left of the column you select.

1 To select a column, move the mouse over the column letter (example: **column B**) and then press the left button.

2 Move the mouse anywhere over the selected column and then press the **right** button. A menu appears.

3 Move the mouse over **Insert** and then press the left button.

◆ Lotus inserts a column and shifts all existing data to the right.

DELETE A ROW OR COLUMN

You can delete a row or column from your worksheet.

Delete a Row

1 To select the row you want to delete, move the mouse ⟆ over the row number (example: **row 4**) and then press the left button.

2 Move the mouse ⟆ anywhere over the selected row and then press the **right** button. A menu appears.

3 Move the mouse ⟆ over **Delete** and then press the left button.

◆ Lotus deletes the row and shifts all existing data upward.

Getting Started	Enter Data	Manage Your Files	Formulas and Functions	**Edit Your Worksheet**	Format Your Worksheet	Print Your Worksheet	Use Multiple Worksheets	Charts	Databases

Change Column Width   **Delete a Row or Column**
Change Row Height   Move Data
Insert a Row or Column   Copy Data

IMPORTANT!

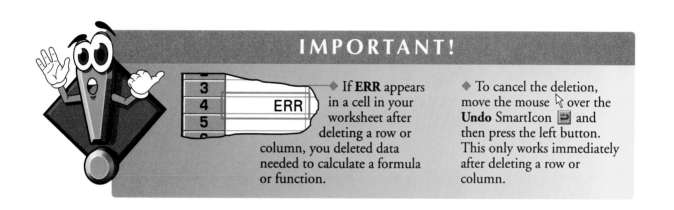

◆ If **ERR** appears in a cell in your worksheet after deleting a row or column, you deleted data needed to calculate a formula or function.

◆ To cancel the deletion, move the mouse ⤢ over the **Undo** SmartIcon 🔁 and then press the left button. This only works immediately after deleting a row or column.

Delete a Column

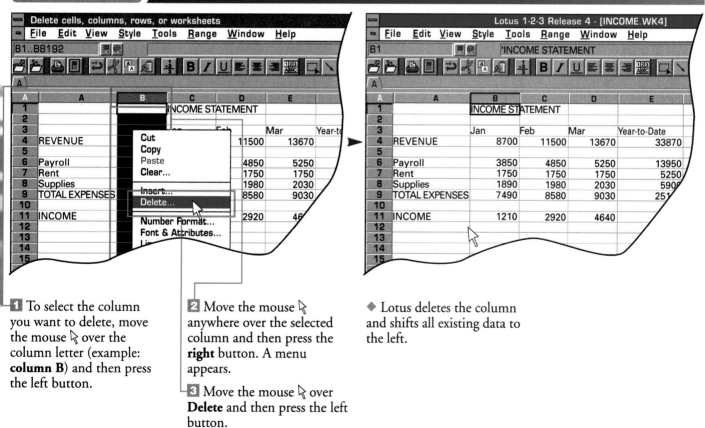

1 To select the column you want to delete, move the mouse ⤢ over the column letter (example: **column B**) and then press the left button.

2 Move the mouse ⤢ anywhere over the selected column and then press the **right** button. A menu appears.

3 Move the mouse ⤢ over **Delete** and then press the left button.

◆ Lotus deletes the column and shifts all existing data to the left.

MOVE DATA

You can move data from one location in your worksheet to another. Lotus "cuts" the data and "pastes" it in a new location. The original data disappears.

Move Data

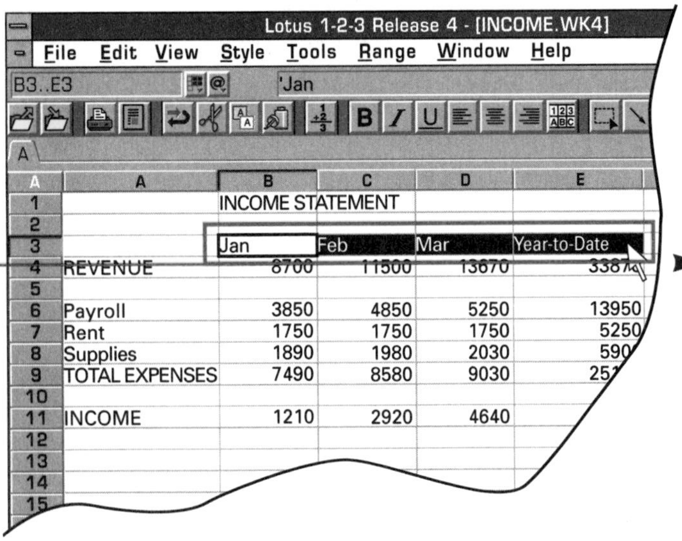

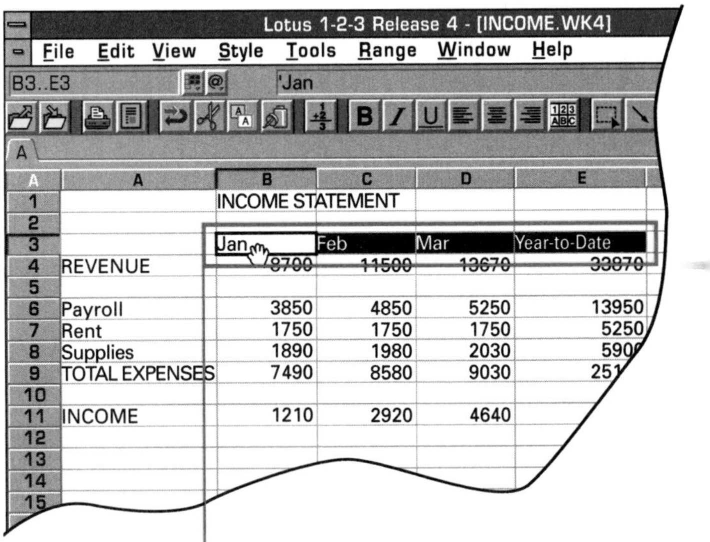

1 Select the cells containing the data you want to move to a new location (example: **B3** to **E3**).

Note: To select cells, refer to page 16.

2 Move the mouse � over any border of the selected cells and it changes to ✋.

| Getting Started | Enter Data | Manage Your Files | Formulas and Functions | **Edit Your Worksheet** | Format Your Worksheet | Print Your Worksheet | Use Multiple Worksheets | Charts | Databases |

Change Column Width   Delete a Row or Column
Change Row Height   **Move Data**
Insert a Row or Column   Copy Data

TIP

◆ You can also move data to another worksheet.

Note: To move data between worksheets, refer to page 96.

3 Press and hold down the left button and then drag the mouse to where you want to move the data.

◆ A dotted rectangular box indicates the new location.

4 Release the button to move the data.

COPY
DATA

You can copy data from one location in your worksheet to another. Lotus "copies" the data and "pastes" it in a new location. The original data remains in its place.

Copy Data

1 Select the cells containing the data you want to copy to a new location (example: **B13** to **E13**).

Note: To select cells, refer to page 16.

2 Move the mouse ⌖ over any border of the selected cells and it changes to ☜.

| Getting Started | Enter Data | Manage Your Files | Formulas and Functions | **Edit Your Worksheet** | Format Your Worksheet | Print Your Worksheet | Use Multiple Worksheets | Charts | Databases |

Change Column Width   Delete a Row or Column
Change Row Height   Move Data
Insert a Row or Column   **Copy Data**

♦ You can also copy data to another worksheet.

Note: To copy data between worksheets, refer to page 96.

Lotus 1-2-3 Release 4 - [INCOME.WK4]

File Edit View Style Tools Range Window Help

B13..E13   'Jan

	A	B	C	D	E	F
1		INCOME STATEMENT				
2						
3						
4	REVENUE	6700	11500	13670	33870	
5						
6	Payroll	3850	4850	5250	13950	
7	Rent	1750	1750	1750	5250	
8	Supplies	1890	1980	2030	5900	
9	TOTAL EXPENSES	7490	8580	9030	25100	
10						
11	INCOME	210	2920	4640	8770	
12						
13		Jan	Feb	Mar	Year-to-Date	
14						

Lotus 1-2-3 Release 4 - [INCOME.WK4]

File Edit View Style Tools Range Window Help

B3..E3   'Jan

	A	B	C	D	E	F
1		INCOME STATEMENT				
2						
3		Jan	Feb	Mar	Year-to-Date	
4	REVENUE	8700	11500	13670	3387	
5						
6	Payroll	3850	4850	5250	13950	
7	Rent	1750	1750	1750	5250	
8	Supplies	1890	1980	2030	5900	
9	TOTAL EXPENSES	7490	8580	9030	25100	
10						
11	INCOME	1210	2920	4640	8770	
12						
13		Jan	Feb	Mar	Year-to-Date	

3 Press and hold down Ctrl.

4 Still holding down Ctrl, press and hold down the left button and then drag the mouse to where you want to copy the data.

♦ A dotted rectangular box indicates the new location.

5 Release the button, then release Ctrl to copy the data.

CHANGE APPEARANCE OF NUMBERS

To make the numbers in your worksheet easier to read and comprehend, you can change the way they are displayed. Some of the number styles Lotus offers are:

Scientific	1.04E+03
Currency	$1,037.82
, Comma	1,037.82
General	1037.82
Percent	103782.00%

Change Appearance of Numbers

1 Select the cells containing the numbers you want to change.

Note: To select cells, refer to page 16.

2 To display a list of number styles, move the mouse ⟍ over this box and then press the left button. A menu appears.

3 Move the mouse ⟍ over the number style you want to use (example: **Currency**) and then press the left button.

Change Appearance of Numbers
Align Data
Bold, Italics and Underline
Change Fonts
Change Font Size

Add Borders
Style Data Automatically
Draw Arrows and Shapes
Display Different SmartIcons

DATES

You can change the way dates are displayed in your worksheet using the method described below. Some options are:

31-Dec-93

31-Dec

Dec-93

12/31/93

12/31

TIMES

You can change the way times are displayed in your worksheet using the method described below. Some options are:

11:59:59 AM

11:59 AM

23:59:59

23:59

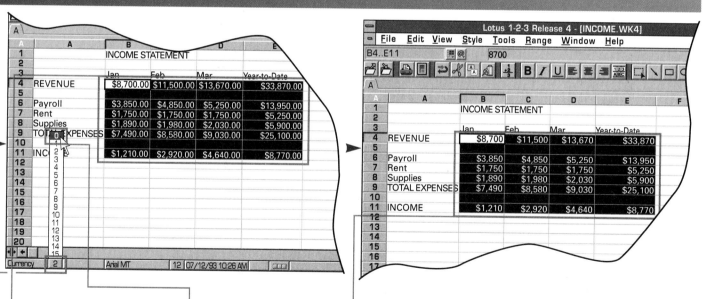

◆ The numbers are now displayed in the new style.

4 To change the number of decimal places, move the mouse ⓡ over this box and then press the left button. A menu appears.

5 Move the mouse ⓡ over the number of decimal places you want to display (example: **0**) and then press the left button.

◆ The numbers are now displayed with the number of decimal places you selected.

Note: If asterisks (***) appear in a cell, the column width is not wide enough to display the number. To display the entire number, change the column width. For more information, refer to page 48.

ALIGN
DATA

You can change the position of the data in each cell of your worksheet. Lotus offers three alignment options.

Data		**Left Align**
Data		**Center**
Data		**Right Align**

Center Data

1 Select the cells containing the data you want to center (example: **B3** to **E3**).

Note: To select cells, refer to page 16.

2 Move the mouse ⟶ over the **Center** SmartIcon and then press the left button.

◆ Lotus centers the data in the selected cells.

Getting Started	Enter Data	Manage Your Files	Formulas and Functions	Edit Your Worksheet	**Format Your Worksheet**	Print Your Worksheet	Use Multiple Worksheets	Charts	Databases

Change Appearance of Numbers Add Borders
Align Data Style Data Automatically
Bold, Italics and Underline Draw Arrows and Shapes
Change Fonts Display Different SmartIcons
Change Font Size

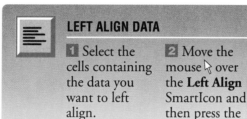

LEFT ALIGN DATA

1 Select the cells containing the data you want to left align.

2 Move the mouse ⇱ over the **Left Align** SmartIcon and then press the left button.

Right Align Data

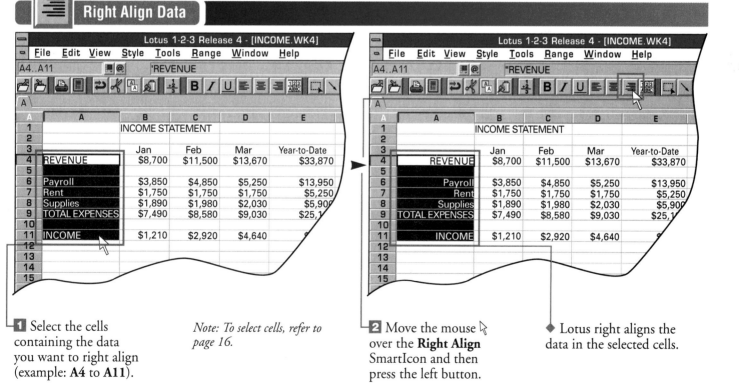

1 Select the cells containing the data you want to right align (example: **A4** to **A11**).

Note: To select cells, refer to page 16.

2 Move the mouse ⇱ over the **Right Align** SmartIcon and then press the left button.

◆ Lotus right aligns the data in the selected cells.

BOLD, ITALICS AND UNDERLINE

You can use the Bold, Italic and Underline SmartIcons to emphasize important information. This will improve the overall appearance of your worksheet.

bold   *italic*   underline

B Bold Data

Lotus 1-2-3 Release 4 - [INCOME.WK4]

File Edit View Style Tools Range Window Help

B3..E3   ^Jan

	A	B	C	D	E
1		INCOME STATEMENT			
2					
3			Jan	Feb	Mar	Year-to-Date
4	REVENUE	$8,700	$11,500	$13,670	$33,870
5					
6	Payroll	$3,850	$4,850	$5,250	$13,950
7	Rent	$1,750	$1,750	$1,750	$5,250
8	Supplies	$1,890	$1,980	$2,030	$5,9
9	TOTAL EXPENSES	$7,490	$8,580	$9,030	$25
10					
11	INCOME	$1,210	$2,920	$4,640	
12					
13					

Lotus 1-2-3 Release 4 - [INCOME.WK4]

File Edit View Style Tools Range Window Help

B3..E3   ^Jan

	A	B	C	D	E
1		INCOME STATEMENT			
2					
3			**Jan**	**Feb**	**Mar**	**Year-to-Date**
4	REVENUE	$8,700	$11,500	$13,670	$33,870
5					
6	Payroll	$3,850	$4,850	$5,250	$13,950
7	Rent	$1,750	$1,750	$1,750	$5,25
8	Supplies	$1,890	$1,980	$2,030	$5,9
9	TOTAL EXPENSES	$7,490	$8,580	$9,030	$25
10					
11	INCOME	$1,210	$2,920	$4,640	

1 Select the cells containing the data you want to bold (example: **B3** to **E3**).

Note: To select cells, refer to page 16.

2 Move the mouse ⏸ over the **Bold** SmartIcon and then press the left button.

◆ The data in the selected cells appears in the bold style.

Note: To remove the bold style, repeat steps 1 and 2.

64

I Italicize Data

Lotus 1-2-3 Release 4 - [INCOME.WK4]

File Edit View Style Tools Range Window Help

A4..A11   "REVENUE

	A	B	C	D	E
1		INCOME STATEMENT			
2					
3		Jan	Feb	Mar	Year-to-Date
4	*REVENUE*	$8,700	$11,500	$13,670	$33,870
5					
6	*Payroll*	$3,850	$4,850	$5,250	$13,950
7	*Rent*	$1,750	$1,750	$1,750	$5,250
8	*Supplies*	$1,890	$1,980	$2,030	$5,9
9	*TOTAL EXPENSES*	$7,490	$8,580	$9,030	$25
10					
11	*INCOME*	$1,210	$2,920	$4,640	
12					
13					
14					

1 Select the cells containing the data you want to italicize (example: **A4** to **A11**).

Note: To select cells, refer to page 16.

2 Move the mouse ⩗ over the **Italic** SmartIcon and then press the left button.

◆ The data in the selected cells appears in italics.

*Note: To remove the italic style, repeat steps **1** and **2**.*

U Underline Data

Lotus 1-2-3 Release 4 - [INCOME.WK4]

File Edit View Style Tools Range Window Help

B1   'INCOME STATEMENT

	A	B	C	D	E
1		INCOME STATEMENT			
2					
3		Jan	Feb	Mar	Year-to-Date
4	*REVENUE*	$8,700	$11,500	$13,670	$33,870
5					
6	*Payroll*	$3,850	$4,850	$5,250	$13,950
7	*Rent*	$1,750	$1,750	$1,750	$5,25
8	*Supplies*	$1,890	$1,980	$2,030	$5,9
9	*TOTAL EXPENSES*	$7,490	$8,580	$9,030	$25
10					
11	*INCOME*	$1,210	$2,920	$4,640	
12					
13					
14					

1 Select the cells containing the data you want to underline (example: **B1**).

Note: To select cells, refer to page 16.

2 Move the mouse ⩗ over the **Underline** SmartIcon and then press the left button.

◆ The data in the selected cells is underlined.

*Note: To remove the underline style, repeat steps **1** and **2**.*

You can change the design of the characters (font) in your worksheet. This enables you to emphasize headings and make data easier to read.

Arial Times Courier

Change Fonts

Lotus 1-2-3 Release 4 - [INC

File   Edit   View   Style   Tools   Range   Window

B1   'INCOME STATEMENT

	A	B	C	D
1		INCOME STATEMENT		
2				
3		Jan	Feb	Mar
4	REVENUE	$8,700	$11,500	$13,6
5				
6	Payroll	$3,850	$4,850	
7	Rent	$1,750	$1,750	
8	Supplies	$1,890	$1,980	
9	TOTAL EXPEN			

1 Select the cells containing the data you want to change to a new font (example: **B1**).

Note: To select cells, refer to page 16.

Change Appearance of Numbers
Align Data
Bold, Italics and Underline
Change Fonts
Change Font Size

Add Borders
Style Data Automatically
Draw Arrows and Shapes
Display Different SmartIcons

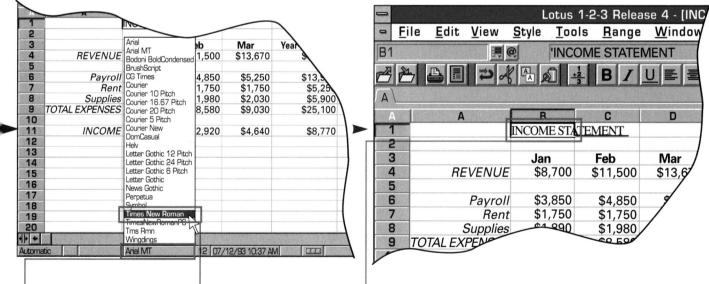

2 Move the mouse ⍨ over this box and then press the left button. A list of fonts appears.

Note: The fonts displayed on your screen may be different than shown above.

3 Move the mouse ⍨ over the font you want to use (example: **Times New Roman**) and then press the left button.

◆ The data in the selected cells displays the new font.

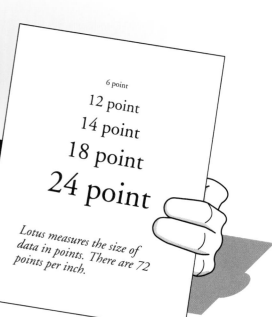

You can emphasize data in your worksheet by increasing or decreasing its size. Lotus offers many different font sizes to choose from.

6 point

12 point

14 point

18 point

24 point

Lotus measures the size of data in points. There are 72 points per inch.

Change Font Size

Lotus 1-2-3 Release 4 - [INCOME.WK4]

File   Edit   View   Style   Tools   Range   Window   Help

A4   "REVENUE

	A	B	C	D	E
1		INCOME STATEMENT			
2					
3		Jan	Feb	Mar	Year-to-Date
4	REVENUE	$8,700	$11,500	$13,670	$33,870
5					
6	Payroll	$3,850	$4,850	$5,250	$13,950
7	Rent	$1,750	$1,750	$1,750	$5,250
8	Supplies	$1,890	$1,980	$2,030	$5,90
9	TOTAL EXPENSES	$7,490	$8,580	$9,030	$25,
10					
11	INCOME	$1,210	$2,920	$4,640	
12					
13					
14					
15					

1 Select the cells containing the data you want to change to a new font size (example: **A4**).

Note: To select cells, refer to page 16.

Change Appearance of Numbers   Add Borders
Align Data   Style Data Automatically
Bold, Italics and Underline   Draw Arrows and Shapes
Change Fonts   Display Different SmartIcons
Change Font Size

Left worksheet

A		Jan	Feb	Mar	Year-
1	INCO...				
4	REVENUE	$8,700	$11,500	$13,670	$3...
6	Payroll	$3,850	$4,850	$5,250	$13,9...
7	Rent	$1,750	$1,750	$1,750	$5,250
8	Supplies	$1,890	$1,980	$2,030	$5,900
9	TOTAL EXPENSES	$7,490	$8,580	$9,030	$25,100
11	INCOME	$1,210	$2,920	$4,640	$8,770

Font size list: 6, 8, 10, 12, 14, **18**, 24, 32, 48, 72

Status bar: Automatic   Arial MT   12   07/12/93 10:40 AM

Right worksheet

Lotus 1-2-3 Release 4 - [INCOME.WK4]

File Edit View Style Tools Range Window Help

A4   "REVENUE

	A	B	C	D	E
1		INCOME STATEMENT			
3		Jan	Feb	Mar	Year-to-Date
4	*REVENUE*	$8,700	$11,500	$13,670	$33,870
6	Payroll	$3,850	$4,850	$5,250	$13,950
7	Rent	$1,750	$1,750	$1,750	$5,250
8	Supplies	$1,890	$1,980	$2,030	$5,9...
9	TOTAL EXPENSES	$7,490	$8,580	$9,030	$25...
11	INCOME	$1,210	$2,920	$4,640	

2 Move the mouse over this box and then press the left button. A list of font sizes appears.

3 Move the mouse over the font size you want to use (example: **18**) and then press the left button.

◆ Lotus changes the size of the data in the selected cells.

◆ The program automatically adjusts the row height to fit the new size.

ADD
BORDERS

To draw attention to data, you can place borders around cells in your worksheet. Lotus offers several types of borders.

Add Borders

1 Select the cells you want to display borders (example: **A4** to **A11**).

Note: To select cells, refer to page 16.

2 Move the mouse ⍽ anywhere over the selected cells and then press the **right** button. A menu appears.

3 Move the mouse ⍽ over **Lines & Color** and then press the left button.

◆ The **Lines & Color** dialog box appears.

4 Move the mouse ⍽ over the type of border you want to use (example: **Outline**) and then press the left button. ☐ becomes ☒.

Note: To deselect your choice, repeat step 4.

5 To select a line style, move the mouse ⍽ over the arrow beside **Line style:** and then press the left button.

Change Appearance of Numbers
Align Data
Bold, Italics and Underline
Change Fonts
Change Font Size

Add Borders
Style Data Automatically
Draw Arrows and Shapes
Display Different SmartIcons

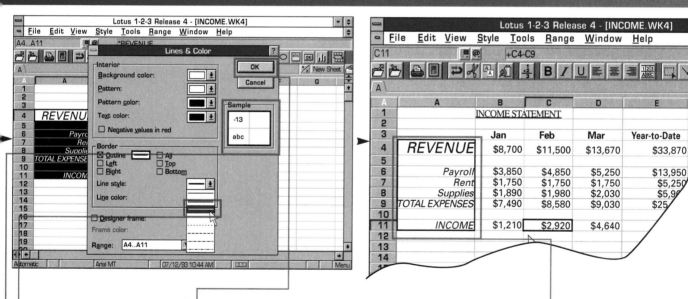

6 Move the mouse ⇱ over the line style you want to use and then press the left button.

◆ A sample of the border you selected appears.

Note: To select additional borders, repeat steps 4 to 6.

7 Move the mouse ⇱ over **OK** and then press the left button.

8 To view the new border, move the mouse ⇱ over any cell outside the selected area (example: **C11**) and then press the left button.

◆ A border appears around the cells you selected.

You can have Lotus automatically style a section of your worksheet to quickly give it a professional look. Lotus provides you with many different styles to choose from.

Style Data Automatically

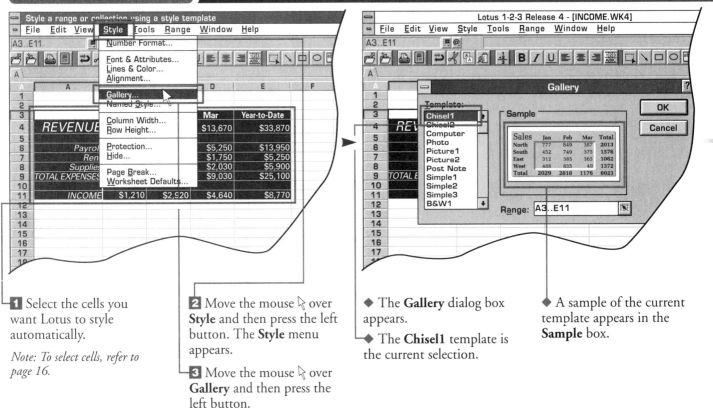

1 Select the cells you want Lotus to style automatically.

Note: To select cells, refer to page 16.

2 Move the mouse ⬦ over **Style** and then press the left button. The **Style** menu appears.

3 Move the mouse ⬦ over **Gallery** and then press the left button.

◆ The **Gallery** dialog box appears.

◆ The **Chisel1** template is the current selection.

◆ A sample of the current template appears in the **Sample** box.

Change Appearance of Numbers
Align Data
Bold, Italics and Underline
Change Fonts
Change Font Size

Add Borders
Style Data Automatically
Draw Arrows and Shapes
Display Different SmartIcons

CLEAR STYLES

You can remove all the styles (example: colors, bolding, alignment) from an area in your worksheet. The data in the cells remains unchanged.

■1 Select the cells containing the styles you want to remove.

■2 Move the mouse ⬚ anywhere over the selected cells and then press the **right** button. A menu appears.

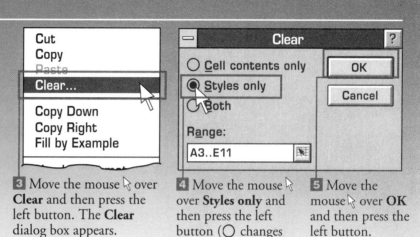

■3 Move the mouse ⬚ over **Clear** and then press the left button. The **Clear** dialog box appears.

■4 Move the mouse ⬚ over **Styles only** and then press the left button (○ changes to ◉).

■5 Move the mouse ⬚ over **OK** and then press the left button.

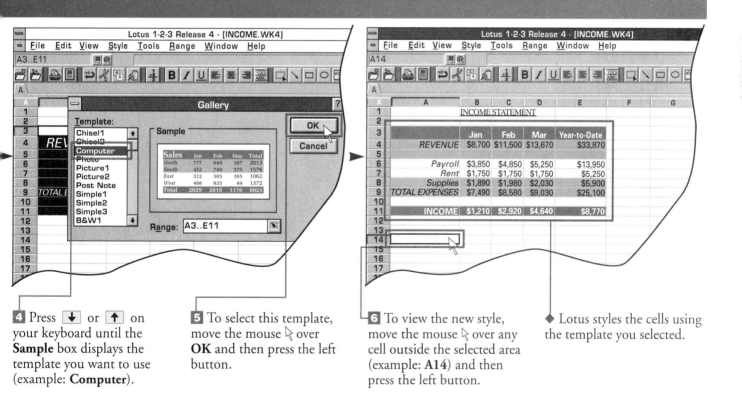

■4 Press ⬇ or ⬆ on your keyboard until the **Sample** box displays the template you want to use (example: **Computer**).

■5 To select this template, move the mouse ⬚ over **OK** and then press the left button.

■6 To view the new style, move the mouse ⬚ over any cell outside the selected area (example: **A14**) and then press the left button.

◆ Lotus styles the cells using the template you selected.

DRAW ARROWS AND SHAPES

You can use your artistic abilities to make your worksheet more meaningful. You can place text in a box, draw arrows, circles and other shapes to draw attention to specific results.

Draw an Arrow

1 Move the mouse ⏳ over the **Arrow** SmartIcon and then press the left button.

◆ The mouse ⏳ changes to ⊹ when you move it over your worksheet.

2 Move the mouse ⊹ where you want to begin drawing the arrow.

3 Press and hold down the left button as you drag the arrow to the desired length.

4 Release the button and the arrow appears.

5 To view the arrow, move the mouse ⏳ over any cell (example: **A14**) and then press the left button.

Change Appearance of Numbers
Align Data
Bold, Italics and Underline
Change Fonts
Change Font Size

Add Borders
Style Data Automatically
Draw Arrows and Shapes
Display Different SmartIcons

DRAW A RECTANGLE OR SQUARE

You can use this SmartIcon to draw a rectangle or square.

1 Move the mouse ⏶ over the SmartIcon and then press the left button.

2 Repeat steps **2** to **4** of "Draw a Text Block" below.

DRAW AN ELLIPSE OR CIRCLE

You can use this SmartIcon to draw an ellipse or circle.

1 Move the mouse ⏶ over the SmartIcon and then press the left button.

2 Repeat steps **2** to **4** of "Draw a Text Block" below.

DELETE AN OBJECT

1 Move the mouse ⏶ over the object until it changes to ⏶ or ⏉.

2 Press the left button and boxes (■) appear around the object.

3 Press **Delete** to remove the object from your worksheet.

Draw a Text Block

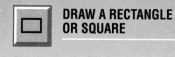
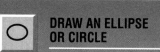
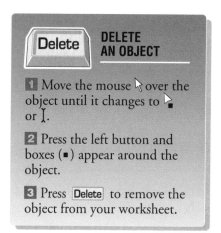

1 Move the mouse ⏶ over the **Text Block** SmartIcon and then press the left button.

◆ The mouse ⏶ changes to ╬ when you move it over your worksheet.

2 Move the mouse ╬ where you want to begin drawing the box.

3 Press and hold down the left button as you drag the box to the desired size.

4 Release the button and the box appears.

5 Type the text you want to appear in the box (example: **GREAT RESULTS!**).

6 To view the text box, move the mouse ⏶ over any cell (example: **A14**) and then press the left button.

DISPLAY DIFFERENT SMARTICONS

SmartIcons enable you to quickly select commonly used commands. Lotus offers a number of SmartIcon sets that you can choose from.

Display Different SmartIcons (Method 1)

	eb	Mar	Year-to-Date
	1,500	$13,670	$33,870
	$4,850	$5,250	$13,950
	750	$1,750	$1,750	$5,250
	,890	$1,980	$2,030	$5,900
	,490	$8,580	$9,030	$25,100
	$1,210	$2,920	$4,640	$8,770

GREAT RESULTS!

Default Sheet
Editing
Formatting
Goodies
Macro Building
Printing
Sheet Auditing
WorkingTogether
Hide SmartIcons

Arial MT   12   07/12/93 10:55 AM   Ready

Lotus 1-2-3 Release 4 - [INCOME.WK4]

File Edit View Style Tools Range Window Help

F13

	A	B	C	D	E	F	G	H
1		INCOME STATEMENT						
2								
3			Jan	Feb	Mar	Year-to-Date		
4	REVENUE	$8,700	$11,500	$13,670	$33,870			
5								
6	Payroll	$3,850	$4,850	$5,250	$13,950			
7	Rent	$1,750	$1,750	$1,750	$5,250			
8	Supplies	$1,890	$1,980	$2,030	$5,900			
9	TOTAL EXPENSES	$7,490	$8,580	$9,030	$25,100			
10								
11	INCOME	$1,210	$2,920	$4,640	$8,770			
12								
13								
14								
15								
16								
17								
18								
19								

GREAT RESULTS!

Automatic   Arial MT   12   07/12/93 10:56 AM   Ready

---

1 Move the mouse ⬚ over this box and then press the left button. A list of available SmartIcon sets appears.

2 Move the mouse ⬚ over the SmartIcon set you want to display (example: **Formatting**) and then press the left button.

◆ The new set of SmartIcons you selected appears at the top of your screen.

Note: Each set contains SmartIcons related to a specific function (example: Editing, Printing).

Getting Started	Enter Data	Manage Your Files	Formulas and Functions	Edit Your Worksheet	**Format Your Worksheet**	Print Your Worksheet	Use Multiple Worksheets	Charts	Databases

Change Appearance of Numbers Add Borders
Align Data Style Data Automatically
Bold, Italics and Underline Draw Arrows and Shapes
Change Fonts **Display Different SmartIcons**
Change Font Size

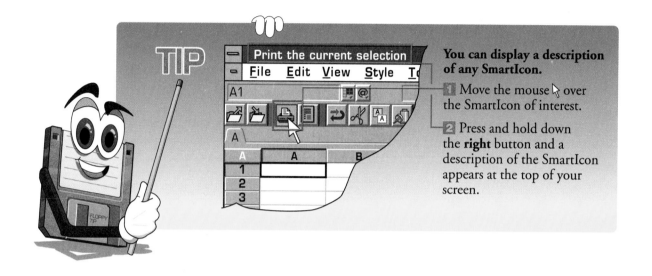

You can display a description of any SmartIcon.

1 Move the mouse over the SmartIcon of interest.

2 Press and hold down the **right** button and a description of the SmartIcon appears at the top of your screen.

Display Different SmartIcons (Method 2)

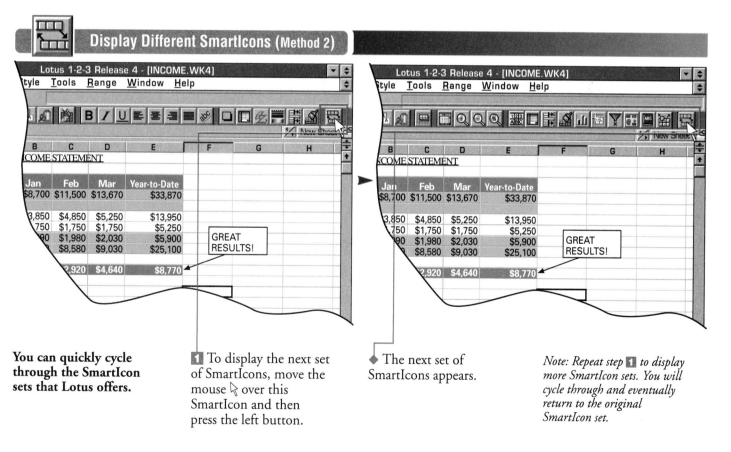

You can quickly cycle through the SmartIcon sets that Lotus offers.

1 To display the next set of SmartIcons, move the mouse over this SmartIcon and then press the left button.

◆ The next set of SmartIcons appears.

Note: Repeat step 1 to display more SmartIcon sets. You will cycle through and eventually return to the original SmartIcon set.

PREVIEW A WORKSHEET

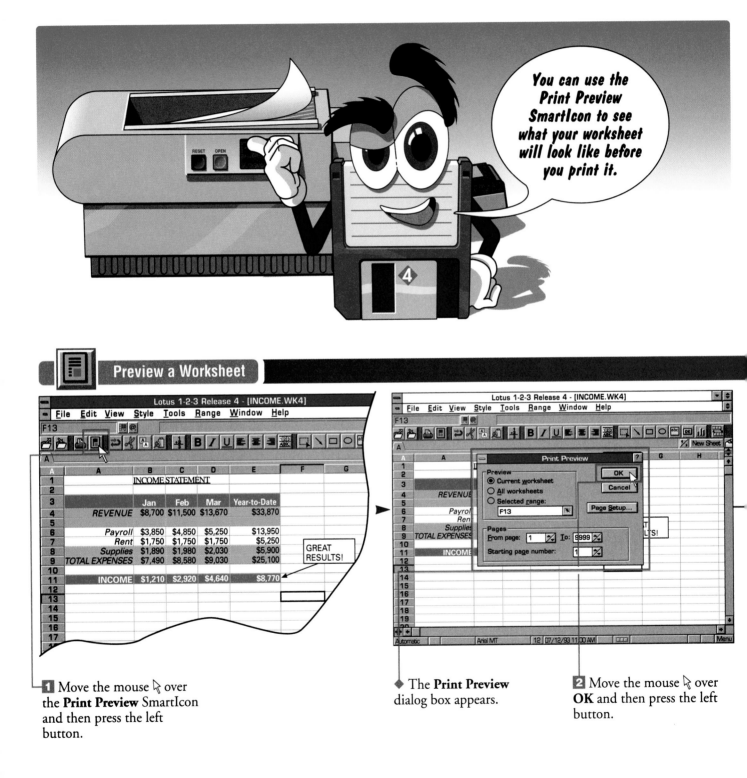

You can use the Print Preview SmartIcon to see what your worksheet will look like before you print it.

Preview a Worksheet

1 Move the mouse ⇗ over the **Print Preview** SmartIcon and then press the left button.

◆ The **Print Preview** dialog box appears.

2 Move the mouse ⇗ over **OK** and then press the left button.

PREVIEW OPTIONS

When previewing your worksheet, you can use the SmartIcons at the top of your screen.

To display the next page, move the mouse ▷ over this SmartIcon and then press the left button.

To display the previous page, move the mouse ▷ over this SmartIcon and then press the left button.

To enlarge the display, move the mouse ▷ over this SmartIcon and then press the left button.

Note: To further enlarge the display, select this SmartIcon again.

To reduce the display, move the mouse ▷ over this SmartIcon and then press the left button.

Note: To further reduce the display, select this SmartIcon again.

To change the page setup, move the mouse ▷ over this SmartIcon and then press the left button. The **Page Setup** dialog box appears.

To print, move the mouse ▷ over this SmartIcon and then press the left button. The **Print** dialog box appears.

To exit **Print Preview** and return to your worksheet, move the mouse ▷ over this SmartIcon and then press the left button.

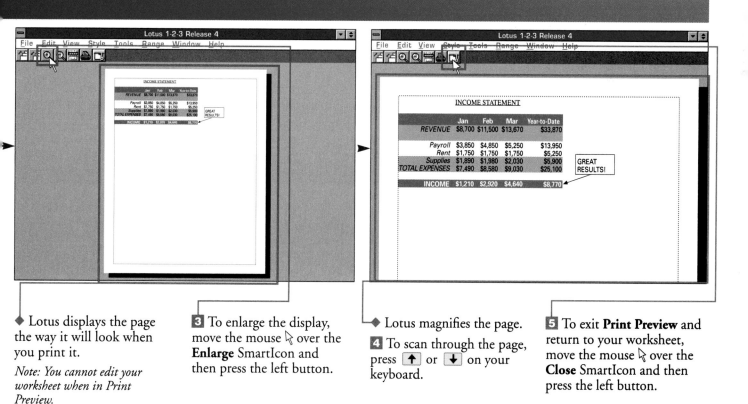

◆ Lotus displays the page the way it will look when you print it.

Note: You cannot edit your worksheet when in Print Preview.

3 To enlarge the display, move the mouse ▷ over the **Enlarge** SmartIcon and then press the left button.

◆ Lotus magnifies the page.

4 To scan through the page, press ⬆ or ⬇ on your keyboard.

5 To exit **Print Preview** and return to your worksheet, move the mouse ▷ over the **Close** SmartIcon and then press the left button.

PRINT A WORKSHEET

When you have finished your worksheet, you can produce a printed copy. You can print a single page, specific pages or your entire worksheet.

Print a Worksheet

1 Move the mouse ⌖ over the **Print** SmartIcon and then press the left button.

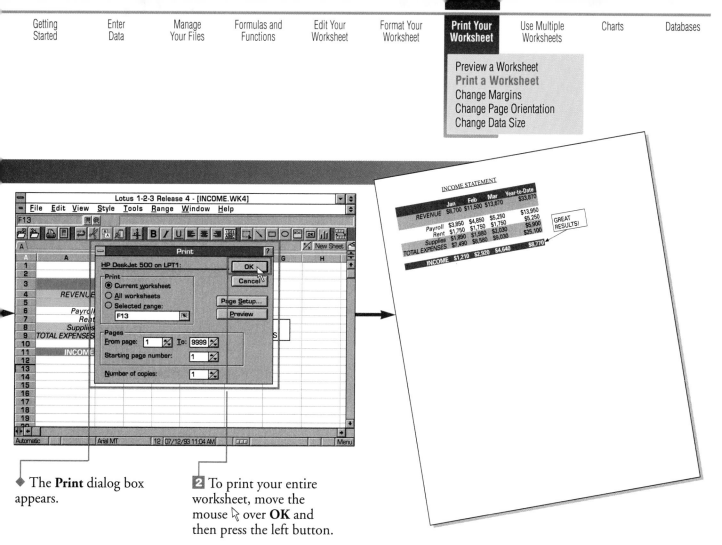

◆ The **Print** dialog box appears.

2 To print your entire worksheet, move the mouse ↖ over **OK** and then press the left button.

Note: To print specific pages, see below.

PRINT SPECIFIC PAGES

You can print specific pages of your worksheet by changing the settings in the Print dialog box.

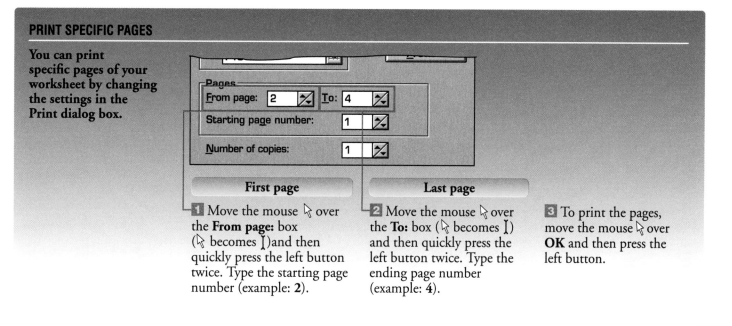

First page

1 Move the mouse ↖ over the **From page:** box (↖ becomes I) and then quickly press the left button twice. Type the starting page number (example: **2**).

Last page

2 Move the mouse ↖ over the **To:** box (↖ becomes I) and then quickly press the left button twice. Type the ending page number (example: **4**).

3 To print the pages, move the mouse ↖ over **OK** and then press the left button.

CHANGE MARGINS

A margin is the amount of space between the printed worksheet and the edges of your paper.

Lotus automatically sets a 0.5 inch margin on the Left, Right, Top and Bottom edges of your paper. You can change these settings.

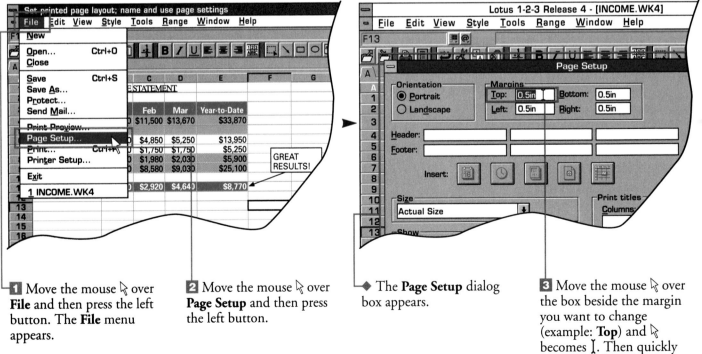

1 Move the mouse ⌖ over **File** and then press the left button. The **File** menu appears.

2 Move the mouse ⌖ over **Page Setup** and then press the left button.

◆ The **Page Setup** dialog box appears.

3 Move the mouse ⌖ over the box beside the margin you want to change (example: **Top**) and ⌖ becomes Ⅰ. Then quickly press the left button twice.

SHOW WORKSHEET FRAME AND GRID LINES

You can print the worksheet frame and grid lines by changing the settings in the Page Setup dialog box.

*Note: To open the **Page Setup** dialog box, perform steps 1 and 2 of "Change Margins" below.*

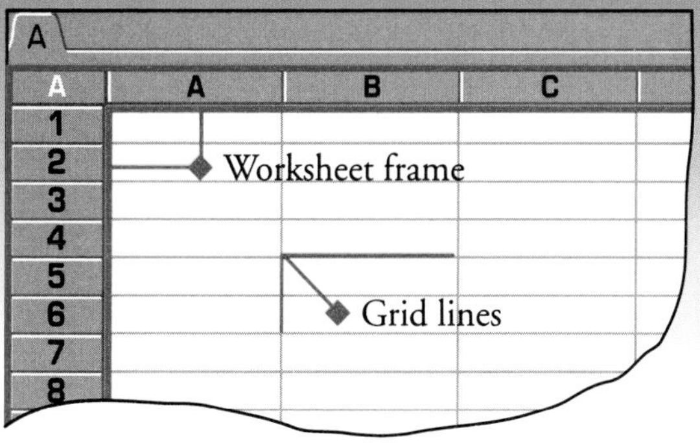

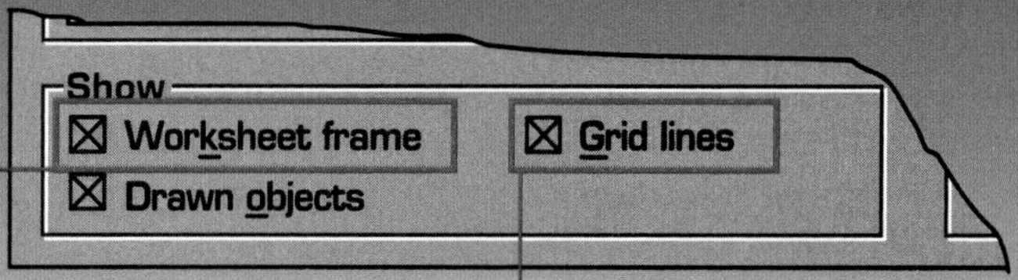

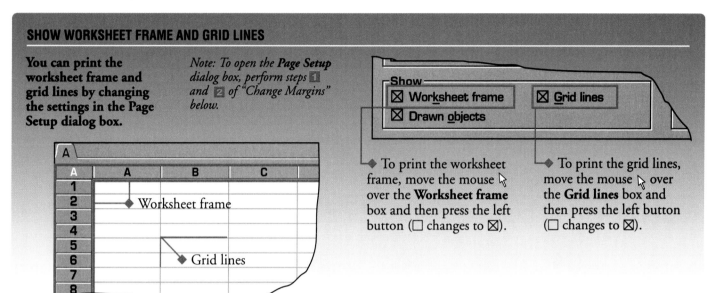

◆ To print the worksheet frame, move the mouse ↖ over the **Worksheet frame** box and then press the left button (☐ changes to ☒).

◆ To print the grid lines, move the mouse ↖ over the **Grid lines** box and then press the left button (☐ changes to ☒).

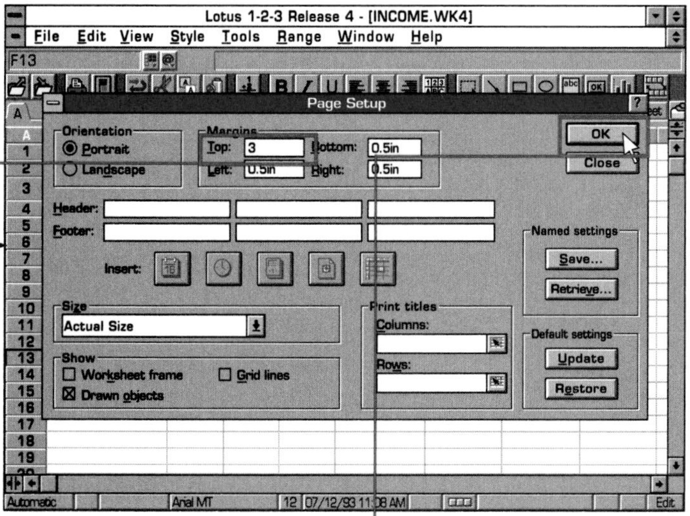

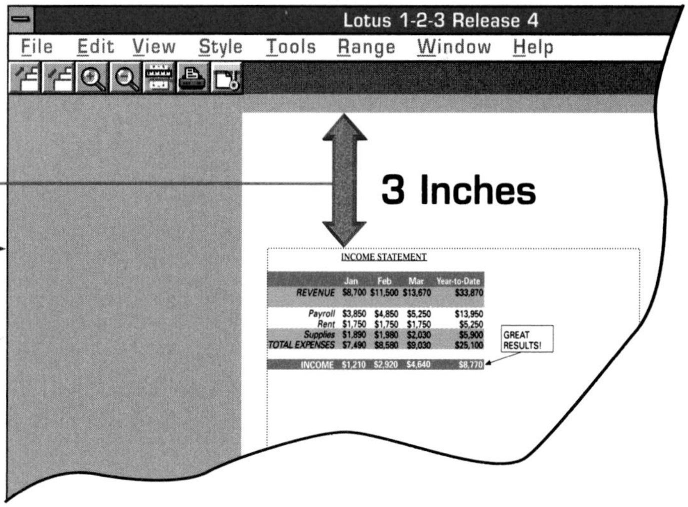

4 Type a new margin in inches (example: **3**).

*Note: Repeat steps **3** and **4** for each margin you want to change.*

5 To confirm the change and return to your worksheet, move the mouse ↖ over **OK** and then press the left button.

◆ You can preview your worksheet to view the new margins.

Note: To preview your worksheet, refer to page 78.

CHANGE PAGE ORIENTATION

If your worksheet is too wide to fit on one page, you may want to change its print orientation. You can use the landscape orientation to print your worksheet across the long side of the page.

Change Page Orientation

Set printed page layout; name and use page settings

| File | Edit | View | Style | Tools | Range | Window | Help |

New
Open...   Ctrl+O
Close

Save   Ctrl+S
Save As...
Protect...
Send Mail...

Print Preview...
Page Setup...
Print...   Ctrl+A
Printer Setup...

Exit

1 INCOME.WK4

	C	D	E	F	G
	E STATEMENT				
	Feb	Mar	Year-to-Date		
	$11,500	$13,670	$33,870		
	$4,850	$5,250	$13,950		
	$1,750	$1,750	$5,250		
	$1,980	$2,030	$5,900	GREAT	
	$8,580	$9,030	$25,100	RESULTS!	
	$2,920	$4,640	$8,770		

1 Move the mouse ⌖ over **File** and then press the left button. The **File** menu appears.

2 Move the mouse ⌖ over **Page Setup** and then press the left button.

Getting Started	Enter Data	Manage Your Files	Formulas and Functions	Edit Your Worksheet	Format Your Worksheet	**Print Your Worksheet**	Use Multiple Worksheets	Charts	Databases

Preview a Worksheet
Print a Worksheet
Change Margins
Change Page Orientation
Change Data Size

PORTRAIT

This is the standard orientation. The worksheet prints across the short side of the paper.

LANDSCAPE

The landscape orientation positions the page so that the long side is horizontal. The data prints across the long side of the paper.

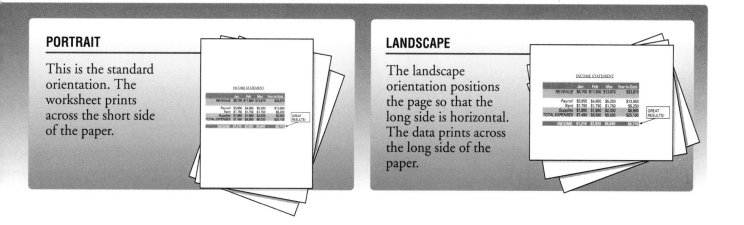

◆ The **Page Setup** dialog box appears.

3 To change to the Landscape orientation, move the mouse ⇧ over **Landscape** and then press the left button (○ becomes ◉).

4 To confirm the change and return to your worksheet, move the mouse ⇧ over **OK** and then press the left button.

◆ You can preview your worksheet to view the new page orientation.

Note: To preview your worksheet, refer to page 78.

CHANGE DATA SIZE

You can decrease or increase the print size. This feature is useful if you want to print your entire worksheet on a single page, even though it normally would not fit.

Change Data Size

1 Move the mouse ⟍ over **File** and then press the left button. The **File** menu appears.

2 Move the mouse ⟍ over **Page Setup** and then press the left button.

◆ The **Page Setup** dialog box appears.

3 Move the mouse ⟍ over the **Size** arrow and then press the left button. A list of size options appears.

Preview a Worksheet
Print a Worksheet
Change Margins
Change Page Orientation
Change Data Size

SIZE OPTIONS

Actual Size .... Lotus prints your worksheet in the standard print size.

Fit all to page .... Lotus reduces the print size so that your worksheet will print on a single page.

Fit columns to page .... Lotus reduces the print size so that all of the columns in your worksheet print on one page.

Fit rows to page .... Lotus reduces the print size so that all of the rows in your worksheet print on one page.

Manually scale .... Lotus reduces or expands the print size according to the percentage you enter.

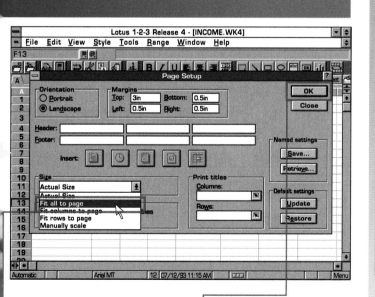

■4 Move the mouse ↖ over the size option you want to use (example: **Fit all to page**) and then press the left button.

*Note: If you select **Manually scale**, see "To Manually Scale Your Data" to the right.*

■5 To confirm the change and return to your worksheet, move the mouse ↖ over **OK** and then press the left button.

TO MANUALLY SCALE YOUR DATA

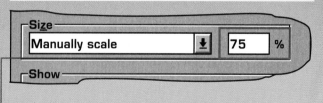

◆ This box appears if you selected **Manually scale** in step ■4.

■1 To specify a percentage, move the mouse ↖ over this box and then quickly press the left button twice.

■2 Type the percentage you want to use (example: **75**).

Note: If the percentage you type is less than 100, Lotus will reduce the print size. If the percentage you type is greater than 100, Lotus will expand the print size.

■3 To confirm the change and return to your worksheet, move the mouse ↖ over **OK** and then press the left button.

CREATE A NEW FILE

SWITCH BETWEEN FILES

You can create a new file to store data on a different topic. Lotus allows you to switch between the current file and any other open files.

Create a New File

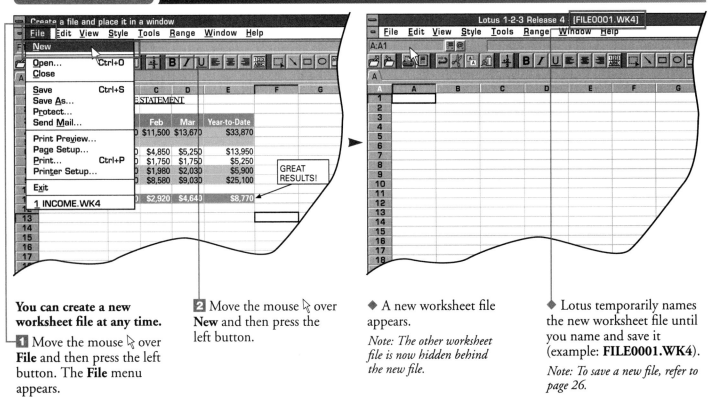

You can create a new worksheet file at any time.

1 Move the mouse ⟷ over **File** and then press the left button. The **File** menu appears.

2 Move the mouse ⟷ over **New** and then press the left button.

◆ A new worksheet file appears.

Note: The other worksheet file is now hidden behind the new file.

◆ Lotus temporarily names the new worksheet file until you name and save it (example: **FILE0001.WK4**).

Note: To save a new file, refer to page 26.

Create a New File   Maximize a File
Switch Between Files   Close a File
Cascade Files   Insert a New Worksheet
Tile Files   Copy/Move Data Between Worksheets

Each worksheet file you create can contain up to 256 worksheets. This enables you to store related worksheets in one location.

Note: To insert a new worksheet in a file, refer to page 94.

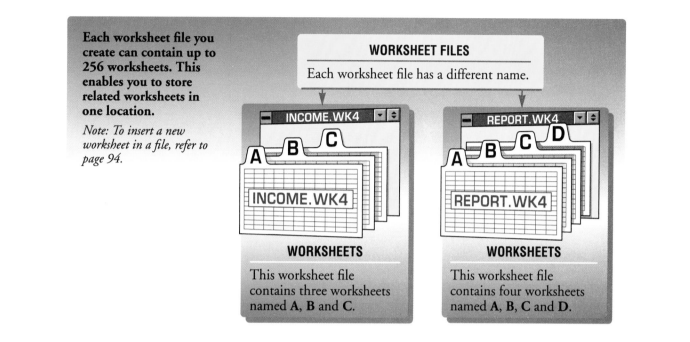

WORKSHEET FILES

Each worksheet file has a different name.

WORKSHEETS

This worksheet file contains three worksheets named **A**, **B** and **C**.

This worksheet file contains four worksheets named **A**, **B**, **C** and **D**.

Switch Between Files

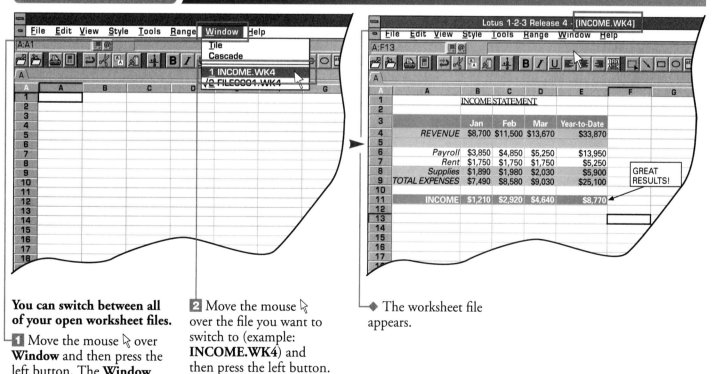

You can switch between all of your open worksheet files.

1 Move the mouse ⌖ over **Window** and then press the left button. The **Window** menu appears.

2 Move the mouse ⌖ over the file you want to switch to (example: **INCOME.WK4**) and then press the left button.

◆ The worksheet file appears.

CASCADE FILES

TILE FILES

If you have several worksheet files open at the same time, some of them may be hidden from view. You can use the Cascade command to display all open worksheet files. Lotus places them one on top of the other.

Cascade Files

1 Move the mouse ℝ over **Window** and then press the left button. The **Window** menu appears.

2 Move the mouse ℝ over **Cascade** and then press the left button.

◆ All of your open worksheet files appear in cascade formation.

Note: The worksheet file you are currently working on appears in front.

Create a New File   Maximize a File
Switch Between Files   Close a File
Cascade Files   Insert a New Worksheet
Tile Files   Copy/Move Data Between Worksheets

Tile Files

1 Move the mouse ▷ over **Window** and then press the left button. The **Window** menu appears.

2 Move the mouse ▷ over **Tile** and then press the left button.

◆ All of your open worksheet files appear in tile formation.

◆ You can only work on the current worksheet which displays a blue title bar.

Note: To work on another worksheet, move the mouse ▷ anywhere over the worksheet and then press the left button.

You may find the current worksheet area too small to effectively work on. You can enlarge (maximize) the current worksheet file to fill your entire screen.

Maximize a File

1 Move the mouse ⬚ over the **Maximize** button of the worksheet file you want to enlarge (example: **FILE0001.WK4**) and then press the left button.

◆ Lotus maximizes the worksheet file to fill your entire screen.

*Note: The **INCOME.WK4** file is hidden behind the current file.*

Getting Started	Enter Data	Manage Your Files	Formulas and Functions	Edit Your Worksheet	Format Your Worksheet	Print Your Worksheet	Use Multiple Worksheets	Charts	Databases

Create a New File   **Maximize a File**
Switch Between Files   **Close a File**
Cascade Files   Insert a New Worksheet
Tile Files   Copy/Move Data Between Worksheets

Close a File

You can close a worksheet file when you are finished working on it.

Note: Lotus will close the current worksheet file.

1 Move the mouse ⇖ over **File** and then press the left button. The **File** menu appears.

2 Move the mouse ⇖ over **Close** and then press the left button.

◆ Lotus closes your worksheet file.

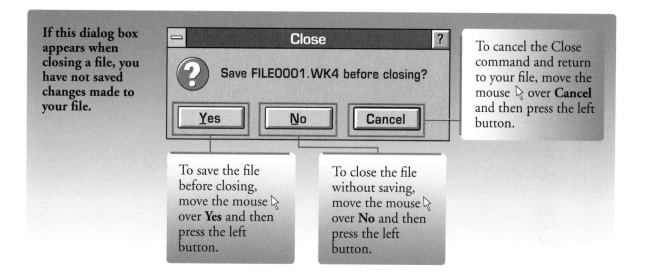

If this dialog box appears when closing a file, you have not saved changes made to your file.

Save FILE0001.WK4 before closing?

[Yes] [No] [Cancel]

To save the file before closing, move the mouse ⇖ over **Yes** and then press the left button.

To close the file without saving, move the mouse ⇖ over **No** and then press the left button.

To cancel the Close command and return to your file, move the mouse ⇖ over **Cancel** and then press the left button.

INSERT A NEW WORKSHEET

You can have up to 256 worksheets in a single file. This enables you to store related worksheets all in one location.

New Sheet | **Insert a New Worksheet**

1 Move the mouse ▷ over **New Sheet** and then press the left button.

◆ Lotus inserts a new worksheet and labels it with a letter (example: **B**).

Create a New File   Maximize a File
Switch Between Files   Close a File
Cascade Files   **Insert a New Worksheet**
Tile Files   Copy/Move Data Between Worksheets

CELL ADDRESS

B: **B3**

◆ This indicates the current worksheet.

◆ This indicates the current cell.

◆ The address of the current cell appears at the top of your screen. The current cell displays a dark border.

DELETE A WORKSHEET

You can permanently remove a worksheet from your file.

Cut
Copy
Paste
Clear...

Insert...
Delete...

Worksheet Defaults...

1 Move the mouse ↖ over the tab of the worksheet you want to delete (example: **B**) and then press the **right** button.

2 Move the mouse ↖ over **Delete** and then press the left button.

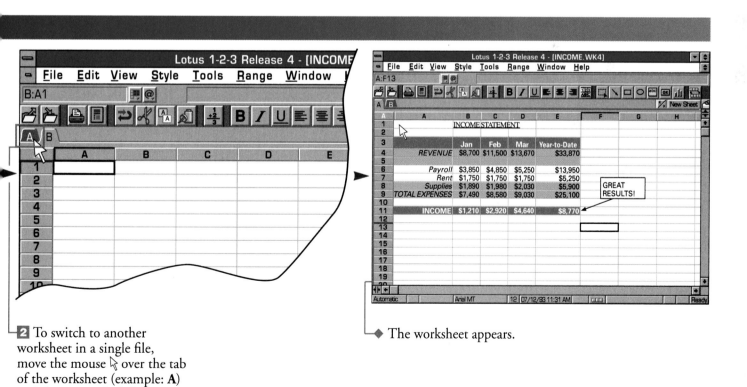

2 To switch to another worksheet in a single file, move the mouse ↖ over the tab of the worksheet (example: **A**) and then press the left button.

◆ The worksheet appears.

95

COPY/MOVE DATA BETWEEN WORKSHEETS

Lotus allows you to copy or move data from one worksheet to another. This can save you time if you are working on a worksheet and want to use data from another file.

INCOME.WK4

FILE0001.WK4

Copy or Move Data Between Worksheets

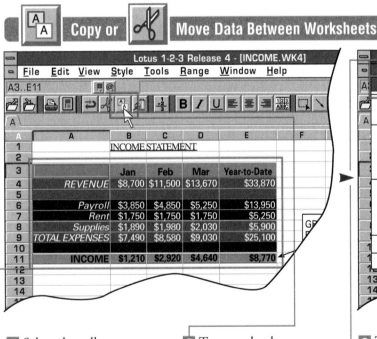

1 Select the cells containing the data you want to copy or move to another worksheet.

Note: To select cells, refer to page 16.

2 To copy the data, move the mouse over the **Copy** SmartIcon and then press the left button.

or

To move the data, move the mouse over the **Cut** SmartIcon and then press the left button.

3 To copy or move the data to a new file, move the mouse over **File** and then press the left button. The **File** menu appears.

Note: You can also copy or move data to a saved file. To open a saved file, refer to page 32.

4 Move the mouse over **New** and then press the left button.

Create a New File   Maximize a File
Switch Between Files   Close a File
Cascade Files   Insert a New Worksheet
Tile Files   **Copy/Move Data Between Worksheets**

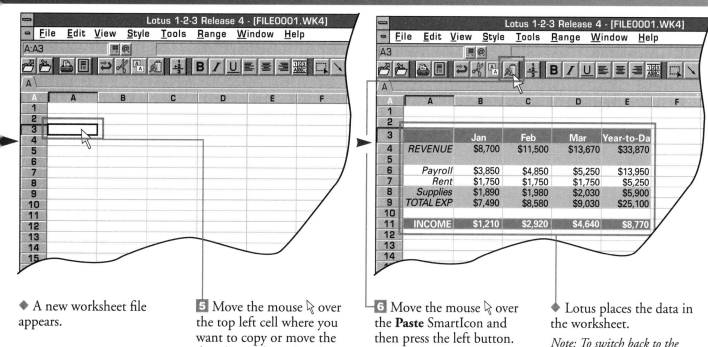

◆ A new worksheet file appears.

5 Move the mouse ⤢ over the top left cell where you want to copy or move the data (example: **A3**) and then press the left button.

6 Move the mouse ⤢ over the **Paste** SmartIcon and then press the left button.

◆ Lotus places the data in the worksheet.

Note: To switch back to the previous file, refer to page 89.

> *You can use a chart to display your worksheet data. Charts make trends or variations easier to visualize. Lotus offers a variety of chart types to choose from.*

Parts of a Chart

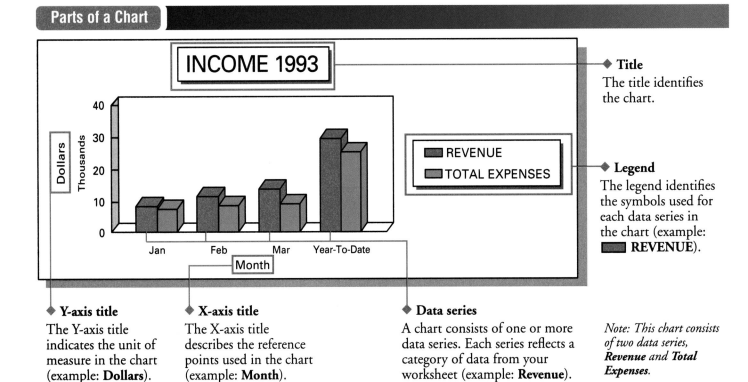

Title
The title identifies the chart.

Legend
The legend identifies the symbols used for each data series in the chart (example: **REVENUE**).

Y-axis title
The Y-axis title indicates the unit of measure in the chart (example: **Dollars**).

X-axis title
The X-axis title describes the reference points used in the chart (example: **Month**).

Data series
A chart consists of one or more data series. Each series reflects a category of data from your worksheet (example: **Revenue**).

Note: This chart consists of two data series, Revenue and Total Expenses.

Chart Types

LINE

Each point on the chart represents a data value. These points are connected with a line. This chart is useful if you want to show data that changes over time (example: sales over the last 10 years).

AREA

An area chart is similar to a line chart except the area below the line is filled in.

BAR

The length of the bars represents the data value. You can use this chart type to represent relationships among data in your worksheet (example: compare revenue and expenses for each month in the year).

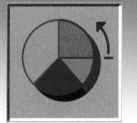

PIE

A pie chart represents each data item as a piece of a pie. This type of chart best illustrates percentages (example: January sales as a percentage of sales for the year).

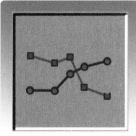

XY

This chart type is often called a scatter chart. You can use this chart to show the relationship between two series of data (example: relationship between education and life-time earnings).

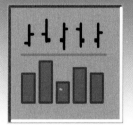

HLCO

A High-Low-Close-Open chart shows the range of values for a series of data. This chart is often called a stock market chart and is best suited for tracing data that fluctuates in a given time period.

MIXED

A mixed chart combines a bar chart with a line or area chart.

RADAR

A radar chart plots data around a central point. You can use this chart to show fluctuations in data (example: each month is an axis, sales for the month are shown as the distance from the center point).

CREATE A CHART

You can create a chart directly from the data in your worksheet.

Create a Chart

1 Select the cells containing the first series of data you want to chart (example: **A3** to **E4**).

Note: To select cells, refer to page 16.

2 To chart a second series of data, press and hold down `Ctrl` while selecting the cells (example: **A9** to **E9**). Then release `Ctrl`.

Note: By selecting the column and row headings in addition to the data, Lotus will automatically create the axis and legend labels.

3 Move the mouse ⌖ over the **Draw a Chart** SmartIcon and then press the left button. The mouse ⌖ changes to when you move it over your worksheet.

Note: To cancel the chart, press `Esc` on your keyboard.

Getting Started	Enter Data	Manage Your Files	Formulas and Functions	Edit Your Worksheet	Format Your Worksheet	Print Your Worksheet	Use Multiple Worksheets	**Charts**	Databases

Introduction   Change Chart Type
Create a Chart   Change Chart Labels
Move a Chart   Change Legend Labels
Size a Chart

TIPS

◆ A chart reflects the data in your worksheet. If you make changes to your worksheet data, the chart automatically updates to display the changes.

◆ You can use arrows and shapes to enhance the appearance of your chart. To draw arrows and shapes, refer to page 74.

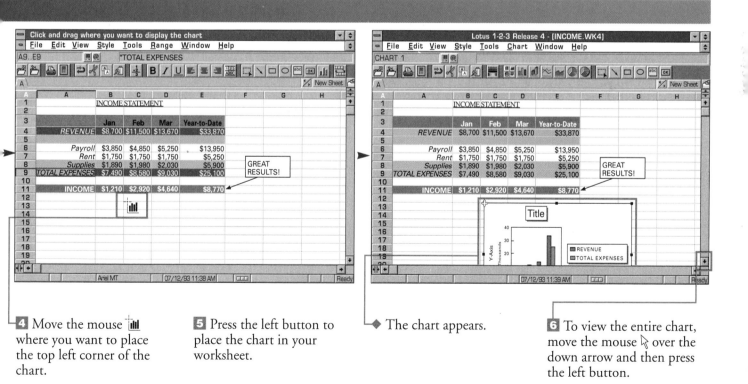

4 Move the mouse 📊 where you want to place the top left corner of the chart.

5 Press the left button to place the chart in your worksheet.

◆ The chart appears.

6 To view the entire chart, move the mouse ▷ over the down arrow and then press the left button.

Move a Chart

1 Move the mouse ⌖ over a blank area in the chart.

Note: The mouse ⌖ changes to ⌖ when it is inside the chart.

2 Press and hold down the left button as you drag the chart to a new location.

◆ A dotted rectangular box indicates the new location.

3 Release the left button to move the chart.

Getting Started	Enter Data	Manage Your Files	Formulas and Functions	Edit Your Worksheet	Format Your Worksheet	Print Your Worksheet	Use Multiple Worksheets	**Charts**	Databases

Introduction
Create a Chart
Move a Chart
Size a Chart

Change Chart Type
Change Chart Labels
Change Legend Labels

PRINT A CHART

You can print a chart without your worksheet data.

1 To select the chart you want to print, move the mouse ⌖ anywhere over the chart and then press the left button.

2 Move the mouse ⌖ over the **Print** SmartIcon and then press the left button. The **Print** dialog box appears.

3 Move the mouse ⌖ over **OK** and then press the left button.

Note: For more information on printing, refer to page 80.

Size a Chart

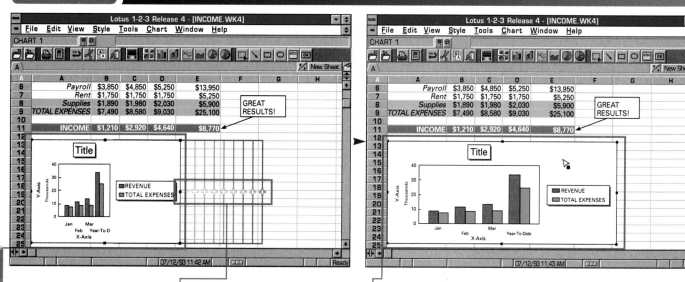

1 To select the chart you want to size, move the mouse ⌖ over the outside edge of the chart and then press the left button.

◆ Boxes (■) appear around the chart.

2 Move the mouse ⌖ over a box (■) and it changes to ⟷.

3 Press and hold down the left button as you drag the side of the chart to the desired size.

4 Release the left button and the new chart size appears.

Note: You can change the size of the chart by using any box (■) around the chart. A corner box will change the length and width of the chart at the same time.

CHANGE CHART TYPE

When you first create a chart, Lotus automatically creates a bar chart. You can easily change the chart type to better suit your worksheet data.

1 To select the chart you want to change, move the mouse ⫯ over the chart and then press the left button.

2 Move the mouse ⫯ over the **Select a Chart Type** SmartIcon and then press the left button. The **Type** dialog box appears.

CHART SMARTICONS

You can instantly change the chart type by moving the mouse ⫯ over one of the above SmartIcons and then pressing the left button.

Getting Started	Enter Data	Manage Your Files	Formulas and Functions	Edit Your Worksheet	Format Your Worksheet	Print Your Worksheet	Use Multiple Worksheets	**Charts**	Databases

Introduction
Create a Chart
Move a Chart
Size a Chart

Change Chart Type
Change Chart Labels
Change Legend Labels

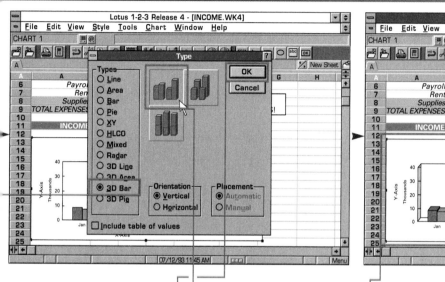

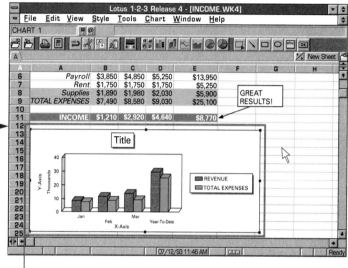

3 Move the mouse ⓀⓀ over the circle beside the chart type you want to use (example: **3D Bar**) and then press the left button.

◆ Lotus displays the available styles for the chart you selected.

4 Move the mouse ⓀⓀ over the style you want to use and then press the left button.

5 To confirm the new chart type, move the mouse ⓀⓀ over **OK** and then press the left button.

◆ The new chart type appears.

CHART ORIENTATION

You can display a chart vertically or horizontally.

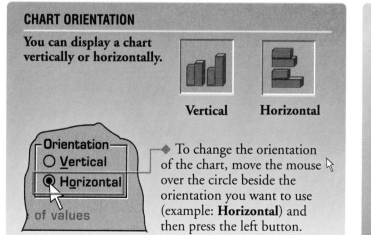

Vertical   **Horizontal**

◆ To change the orientation of the chart, move the mouse ⓀⓀ over the circle beside the orientation you want to use (example: **Horizontal**) and then press the left button.

INCLUDE TABLE OF VALUES

You can display the data used to create the chart in a table. It will appear below the chart.

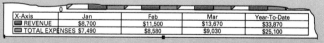

X-Axis	Jan	Feb	Mar	Year-To-Date
REVENUE	$8,700	$11,500	$13,670	$33,870
TOTAL EXPENSES	$7,490	$8,580	$9,030	$25,100

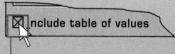

*Note: If **Include table of values** appears dimmed, the option is not available for the chart you selected.*

◆ To include a table of values, move the mouse ⓀⓀ over the box beside **Include table of values** and then press the left button (□ changes to ⊠).

CHANGE
CHART LABELS

You can add a title to your chart and label the x and y axes. This will make your chart more meaningful.

Change Chart Title

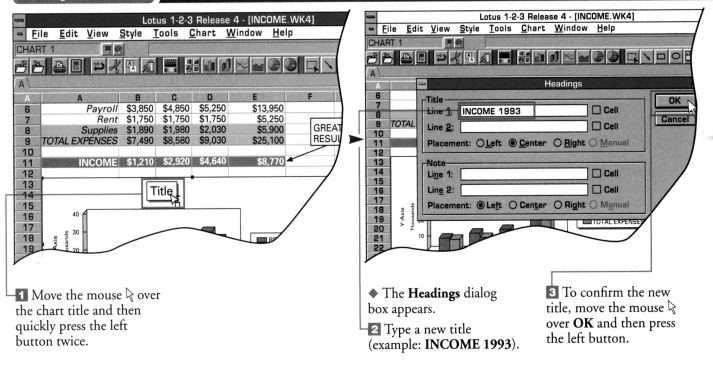

1 Move the mouse ⇧ over the chart title and then quickly press the left button twice.

◆ The **Headings** dialog box appears.

2 Type a new title (example: **INCOME 1993**).

3 To confirm the new title, move the mouse ⇧ over **OK** and then press the left button.

CHANGE AXIS TITLE

X-Axis

Axis title:
Month

☐ Cell

OK

Cancel

Scale manually

0

You can change an axis title.

1 Move the mouse ⌖ over the axis title you want to change (example: **X-Axis**) and then quickly press the left button twice. A dialog box appears.

2 Type a new axis title (example: **Month**).

3 Move the mouse ⌖ over **OK** and then press the left button.

Lotus 1-2-3 Release 4 - [INCOME.WK4]

File Edit View Style Tools Chart Window Help

CHART 1

	A	B	C	D	E	F
6	Payroll	$3,850	$4,850	$5,250	$13,950	
7	Rent	$1,750	$1,750	$1,750	$5,250	
8	Supplies	$1,890	$1,980	$2,030	$5,900	GREAT RESU
9	TOTAL EXPENSES	$7,490	$8,580	$9,030	$25,100	
10						
11	INCOME	$1,210	$2,920	$4,640	$8,770	

INCOME 1993

◆ The new title appears.

CHANGE
LEGEND LABELS

You can change the legend labels for the chart displayed in your worksheet. A legend identifies the symbols used for each series of data in your chart.

Change Legend Labels

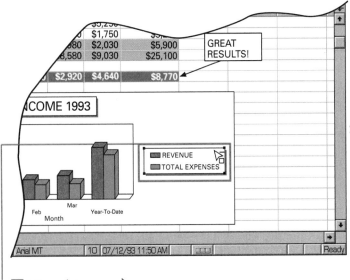

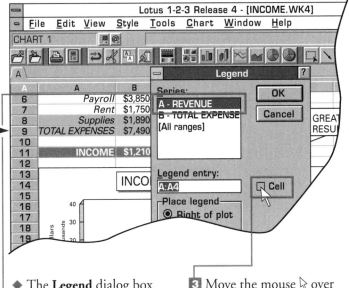

1 Move the mouse ☖ over the legend box and then quickly press the left button twice.

◆ The **Legend** dialog box appears.

2 Move the mouse ☖ over the legend label you want to change (example: **A - REVENUE**) and then press the left button.

3 Move the mouse ☖ over the box beside **Cell** and then press the left button (☒ becomes ☐).

DELETE A CHART

You can delete a chart from your worksheet.

1 To select the chart you want to delete, move the mouse ⌀ over the outside edge of the chart and then press the left button. Boxes (■) appear around the chart.

2 Press Delete .

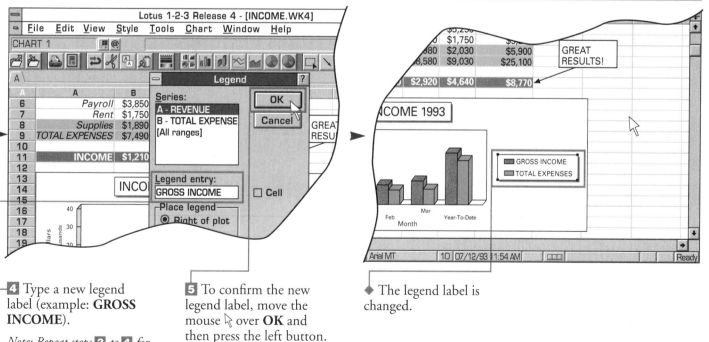

4 Type a new legend label (example: **GROSS INCOME**).

Note: Repeat steps 2 to 4 for each legend label you want to change.

5 To confirm the new legend label, move the mouse ⌀ over **OK** and then press the left button.

◆ The legend label is changed.

SORT INFORMATION

You can change the order that information appears in your database by sorting your data. For example, you can display a list of names and addresses in alphabetical order.

KEEP TRACK OF INFORMATION

You can use a database to help you keep track of your data. A database enables you to maintain an organized and up-to-date listing.

ANALYZE INFORMATION

Lotus allows you to ask questions or "query" the database. You can use the information stored in a database to assist you in making quick and accurate decisions. For example, you can decide if a product line should be discontinued based on an analysis of sales over the last 5 years.

CREATE A DATABASE

You can create a database to store a collection of related information. This will enable you to keep track of your data, sort and search for information.

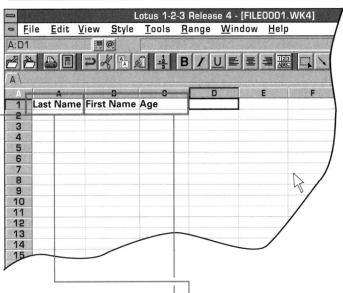

RULES FOR ENTERING FIELD NAMES

◆ A field name must be a label. To enter a field name that begins with a number or non-alphabetic character (example: **1993**), start with a label-prefix (example: **'1993**).

◆ Each field name must be different.

◆ A field name cannot contain the characters **, . : ; - # ~ !** or a blank space.

1 Create a new file.

Note: To create a new file, refer to page 88.

2 Move the mouse ⌖ over the cell where you want the database to begin (example: **A1**) and then press the left button.

3 Type a field name (example: **Last Name**) and then press → to enter the name and move to the next cell.

4 Repeat step **3** to enter the remaining field names.

Note: To bold the field names, refer to page 64. To change the column width, refer to page 48.

RECORDS

◆ A database consists of a collection of records.

◆ A record groups related facts together (example: information on a client).

◆ Each row of information in a Lotus database is a record.

FIELDS

◆ Information within a record is broken down into fields.

◆ A field contains a category of data (example: **Last Name**).

SAVE YOUR DATABASE

You should save your database to permanently store it on your computer.

1 Move the mouse ⇱ over the **Save** SmartIcon and then press the left button. The **Save As** dialog box appears.

2 Type a name for your file (example: **database**).

3 Move the mouse ⇱ over **OK** and then press the left button.

Note: For more information on saving files, refer to page 26.

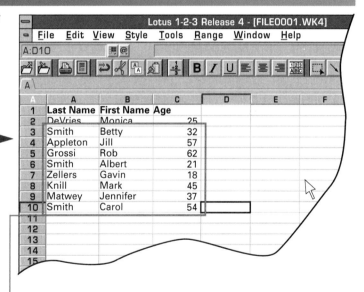

5 Move the mouse ⇱ over the cell directly below the first field name (example: **A2**) and then press the left button.

6 Type the data that corresponds to the field name (example: **DeVries**) and then press → to enter the data and move to the next cell.

7 Repeat step **6** to enter the remaining data for the first record.

8 Type and enter the data for the remaining records.

Note: Do not leave blank rows between records.

FIND RECORDS

You can search for specific records in your database. When Lotus completes the search, it highlights all matching records.

To find specific records in your database, you must specify three items: Field, Operator and Value.

Example:
To find all records with the last name "Smith", you would specify the following:

Field	Operator	Value
Last Name	=	Smith

Find Records

Lotus 1-2-3 Release 4 - [DATABASE.WK4]

File Edit View Style Tools Range Window Help

A1..C10   '@   'Last Name

	A	B	C	D	E	F
1	Last Name	First Name	Age			
2	DeVries	Monica	25			
3	Smith	Betty	32			
4	Appleton	Jill	57			
5	Grossi	Rob	62			
6	Smith	Albert	21			
7	Zellers	Gavin	18			
8	Knill	Mark	45			
9	Matwey	Jennifer	37			
10	Smith	Carol	54			
11						
12						
13						
14						

Locate records in a database table that meet criteria you set

File Edit View Style Tools Range Window Help

A1..C10   '@

Chart
Draw

Database   New Query...

Spell Check...   Find Records...
Audit...   Delete Records...
                  Append Records...
SmartIcons...
User Setup...   Crosstab...

Macro   Connect to External...
Add-in...   Disconnect...
                  Send Command...
                  Create Table...

	A	B	
1	Last Name	First Name	
2	DeVries	Monica	
3	Smith	Betty	
4	Appleton	Jill	
5	Grossi	Rob	
6	Smith	Albert	
7	Zellers	Gavin	
8	Knill	Mark	45
9	Matwey	Jennifer	37
10	Smith	Carol	54
11			
12			
13			
14			
15			
16			

In this example, Lotus will search for all records with the last name "Smith."

1 Select the cells containing the database you want to search. Make sure you include the field names in the selection.

Note: To select cells, refer to page 16.

2 Move the mouse ⌖ over **Tools** and then press the left button. The **Tools** menu appears.

3 Move the mouse ⌖ over **Database** and then press the left button. The **Database** menu appears.

4 Move the mouse ⌖ over **Find Records** and then press the left button.

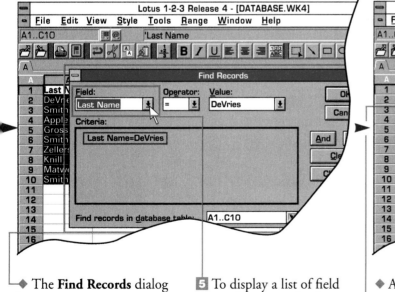

◆ The **Find Records** dialog box appears.

5 To display a list of field names from your database, move the mouse ⟍ over the arrow in the **Field:** box and then press the left button.

◆ A list of field names appears.

6 Move the mouse ⟍ over the field name you want to use in the search (example: **Last Name**) and then press the left button.

Note: To continue the search, refer to the next page.

115

FIND RECORDS

To find specific records in your database, you must specify an operator. Lotus offers six different operators.

OPERATORS

=	finds all records that match
<	finds all records that are lower
>	finds all records that are higher
<=	finds all records that match or are lower
>=	finds all records that match or are higher
<>	finds all records that do not match

Note: Lotus evaluates text alphabetically (example: A is less than B).

Find Records (Continued)

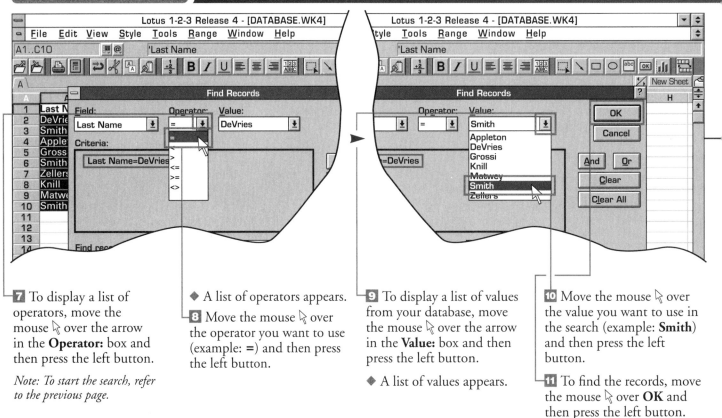

7 To display a list of operators, move the mouse ↔ over the arrow in the **Operator:** box and then press the left button.

Note: To start the search, refer to the previous page.

◆ A list of operators appears.

8 Move the mouse ↔ over the operator you want to use (example: **=**) and then press the left button.

9 To display a list of values from your database, move the mouse ↔ over the arrow in the **Value:** box and then press the left button.

◆ A list of values appears.

10 Move the mouse ↔ over the value you want to use in the search (example: **Smith**) and then press the left button.

11 To find the records, move the mouse ↔ over **OK** and then press the left button.

USING MULTIPLE CRITERIA

You can use AND to combine more than one criteria. This will narrow your search.

◆ **AND** highlights the record if both criteria are met.

Example:

Age > 25 **AND** Last Name = Smith

Lotus will highlight all records of clients older than 25 with the last name Smith.

You can use OR to combine more than one criteria. This will expand your search.

◆ **OR** highlights the record if one or both of the criteria are met.

Example:

Age > 25 **OR** Last Name = Smith

Lotus will highlight all records of clients older than 25 and all clients with the last name Smith.

To specify additional criteria:

1 After completing step **10**, move the mouse ⌖ over **And** or **Or** and then press the left button.

2 To specify another criterion, repeat steps **5** to **10**. Then perform step **11** to execute the search.

Lotus 1-2-3 Release 4 - [DATABASE.WK4]

File   Edit   View   Style   Tools   Range   Window   Help

A10..C10   'Smith

B I U

	A	B	C	D	E	F
1	**Last Name**	**First Name**	**Age**			
2	DeVries	Monica	25			
3	Smith	Betty	32			
4	Appleton	Jill	57			
5	Grossi	Rob	62			
6	Smith	Albert	21			
7	Zellers	Gavin	18			
8	Knill	Mark	45			
9	Matwey	Jennifer	37			
10	Smith	Carol	54			
11						
12						
13						
14						

◆ Lotus highlights all records matching the criteria you specified.

◆ To move from one matching record to another, press Ctrl + Enter.

Note: To remove the highlighting, move the mouse ⌖ over any cell and then press the left button.

SORT DATA

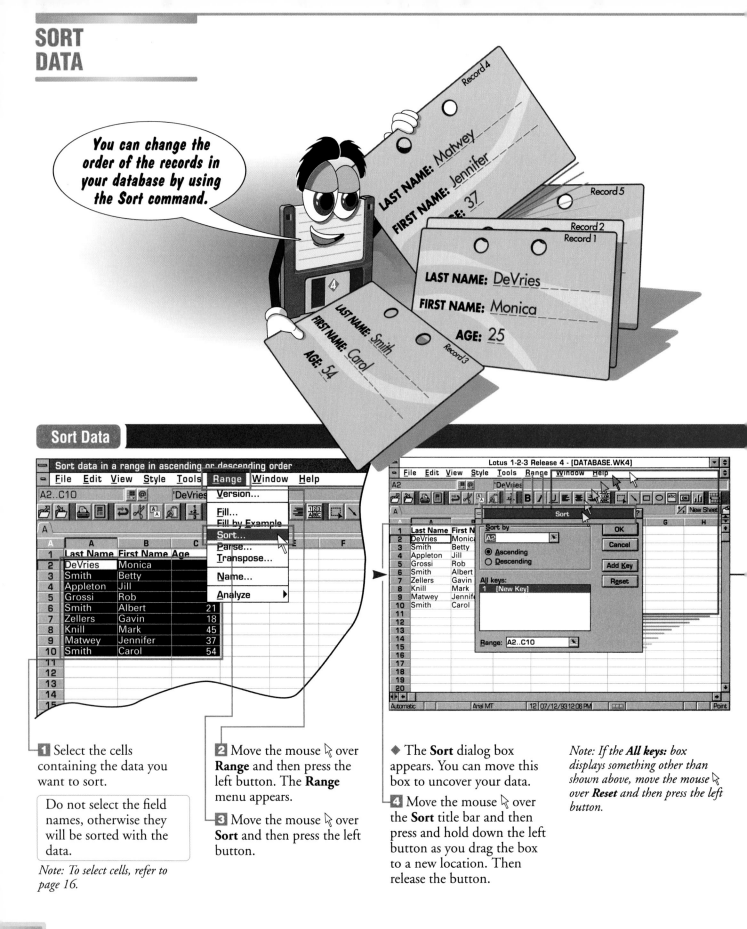

You can change the order of the records in your database by using the Sort command.

Sort Data

1 Select the cells containing the data you want to sort.

Do not select the field names, otherwise they will be sorted with the data.

Note: To select cells, refer to page 16.

2 Move the mouse ⧈ over **Range** and then press the left button. The **Range** menu appears.

3 Move the mouse ⧈ over **Sort** and then press the left button.

◆ The **Sort** dialog box appears. You can move this box to uncover your data.

4 Move the mouse ⧈ over the **Sort** title bar and then press and hold down the left button as you drag the box to a new location. Then release the button.

*Note: If the **All keys:** box displays something other than shown above, move the mouse ⧈ over **Reset** and then press the left button.*

PERFORM A SECONDARY SORT

◆ In this example, the records are alphabetically sorted by last name.

1		
2	Matwey	Jennifer
3	Smith	**Betty**
4	Smith	**Albert**
5	Smith	**Carol**
6	Zellers	Gavin
7		

◆ If a last name appears more than once in your database (example: **Smith**), you can instruct Lotus to perform a secondary sort.

◆ A **secondary sort** by first name arranges the first names in alphabetical order.

1		
2	Matwey	Jennifer
3	Smith	**Albert**
4	Smith	**Betty**
5	Smith	**Carol**
6	Zellers	Gavin
7		

To perform a secondary sort:

1 After completing step **5** below, move the mouse ⌖ over **Add Key** and then press the left button.

2 To specify which column you want to base the secondary sort on, repeat step **5**. Then perform step **6** to execute the sort.

5 Move the mouse ⌖ over any cell in the column you want to base the sort on (example: **A4**) and then press the left button.

◆ Lotus will sort the data in ascending order (A-Z, 0-9).

*Note: To change this order (Z-A, 9-0), move the mouse ⌖ over the circle beside **Descending** and then press the left button (○ becomes ●).*

6 Move the mouse ⌖ over **OK** and then press the left button.

◆ The Last Names are sorted in the order you specified.

You can instruct Lotus to search for specific records in your database and then copy them to another location in your worksheet. This enables you to work with records without making changes to your database.

Extract Records

In this example, Lotus will extract all records of clients 45 years of age or older.

1 Select the cells containing the database you want to extract records from. Make sure you include the field names in the selection.

Note: To select cells, refer to page 16.

2 Move the mouse ⟍ over **Tools** and then press the left button. The **Tools** menu appears.

3 Move the mouse ⟍ over **Database** and then press the left button. The **Database** menu appears.

4 Move the mouse ⟍ over **New Query** and then press the left button.

◆ The **New Query** dialog box appears. You can move this box to uncover your data.

5 Move the mouse ⤢ over the **New Query** title bar and then press and hold down the left button as you drag the box to a new location. Then release the button.

6 Move the mouse ⤢ over the top left cell where you want Lotus to copy the extracted records (example: **A12**) and then press the left button.

7 To define the criteria, move the mouse ⤢ over **Set Criteria** and then press the left button. The **Set Criteria** dialog box appears.

Note: To continue the search, refer to the next page.

EXTRACT RECORDS

> To extract specific records from your database, you must specify three items: Field, Operator and Value.

Example:

To extract all records of clients 45 years of age or older, you would specify the following:

Field	Operator	Value
Age	>=	45

Extract Records (Continued)

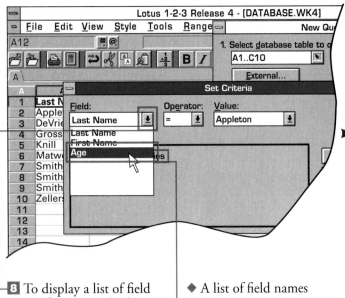

8 To display a list of field names from your database, move the mouse ⬚ over the arrow in the **Field:** box and then press the left button.

Note: To start the search, refer to the previous page.

◆ A list of field names appears.

9 Move the mouse ⬚ over the field name you want to use in the search (example: **Age**) and then press the left button.

10 To display a list of operators, move the mouse ⬚ over the arrow in the **Operator:** box and then press the left button.

Note: For more information on operators, refer to page 116.

◆ A list of operators appears.

11 Move the mouse ⬚ over the operator you want to use (example: **>=**) and then press the left button.

Getting Started	Enter Data	Manage Your Files	Formulas and Functions	Edit Your Worksheet	Format Your Worksheet	Print Your Worksheet	Use Multiple Worksheets	Charts	Databases

Introduction
Create a Database
Find Records
Sort Data
Extract Records

USING MULTIPLE CRITERIA

And You can use AND to combine more than one criteria. This will narrow your search.

◆ **AND** extracts the record if both criteria are met.

Example:

Age > 25 **AND** Last Name = Smith

Lotus will extract all records of clients older than 25 with the last name Smith.

Or You can use OR to combine more than one criteria. This will expand your search.

◆ **OR** extracts the record if one or both of the criteria are met.

Example:

Age > 25 **OR** Last Name = Smith

Lotus will extract all records of clients older than 25 and all clients with the last name Smith.

To specify additional criteria:

1 After completing step **13**, move the mouse ⬚ over **And** or **Or** and then press the left button.

2 To specify another criterion, repeat steps **8** to **13**. Then perform steps **14** and **15** to execute the search.

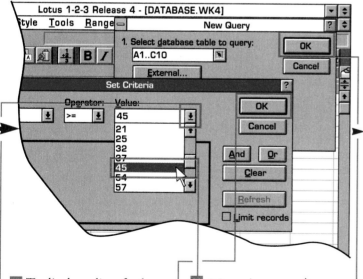

12 To display a list of values from your database, move the mouse ⬚ over the arrow in the **Value:** box and then press the left button.

◆ A list of values appears.

13 Move the mouse ⬚ over the value you want to use in the search (example: **45**) and then press the left button.

14 To return to the **New Query** dialog box, move the mouse ⬚ over **OK** and then press the left button.

15 To extract the records, move the mouse ⬚ over **OK** and then press the left button.

◆ Lotus extracts the records from your database and places them in the location you specified.

INDEX